The Vietnam Plays

THE VIETNAM PLAYS • *Volume Two*

Streamers

The Orphan

DAVID RABE

GROVE PRESS

New York

Published by Grove Press
A division of Grove Press, Inc.
841 Broadway
New York, NY 10003-4793

CAUTION: Professionals and amateurs are hereby warned that
these plays, being fully protected under the Copyright Laws of the
United States of America, the British Commonwealth, including the
Dominion of Canada, and all other countries of the Berne and
Universal Copyright Conventions, are subject to royalty. All rights,
including professional, amateur, recording, motion picture, recita-
tion, lecturing, public reading, radio and television broadcasting,
and the rights of translation into foreign languages, are strictly
reserved, permission for which must be secured in writing from the
author's agent: The Tantleff Office, 375 Greenwich Street, Suite
700, New York, NY 10013. Particular emphasis is laid on the question of readings.

Library of Congress Cataloging-in-Publication Data

Rabe, David.
    The Vietnam plays / by David Rabe. — 1st ed.
        p.   cm.
    Contents: v. 1. The basic training of Pavlo Hummel. Sticks and
bones—v. 2. Streamers. The orphan.
    ISBN 0-8021-3313-4 (v. 1).—ISBN 0-8021-3345-2 (v. 2)
    1. Vietnamese Conflict, 1961–1975—Drama.   I. Title.
PS3568.A23A6   1993
812'.54—dc20   92-37145
                         CIP

Manufactured in the United States of America

Printed on acid-free paper

Designed by Jack Meserole

First Edition 1993

1   3   5   7   9   10   8   6   4   2

CONTENTS

Streamers

For Wyle Walker and Mike Nichols

MASTER SSU, MASTER YÜ, MASTER LI AND MASTER LAI

All at once Master Yü fell ill, and Master Ssu went to ask how he was. "Amazing!" exclaimed Master Yü. "Look, the Creator is making me all crookedy! My back sticks up like a hunchback's so that my vital organs are on top of me. My chin is hidden down around my navel, my shoulders are up above my head, and my pigtail points at the sky. It must be due to some dislocation of the forces of the yin and the yang. . . ."

"Do you resent it?" asked Master Ssu.

"Why, no," replied Master Yü. "What is there to resent . . . ?"

Then suddenly Master Lai also fell ill. Gasping for breath, he lay at the point of death. His wife and children gathered round in a circle and wept. Master Li, who had come to find out how he was, said to them, "Shoooooo! Get back! Don't disturb the process of change."

And he leaned against the doorway and chatted with Master Lai. "How marvelous the Creator is!" he exclaimed. "What is he going to make out of you next? Where is he going to send you? Will he make you into a rat's liver? Will he make you into a bug's arm?"

"A child obeys his father and mother and goes wherever he is told, east or west, south or north," said Master Lai. "And the yin and the yang—how much more are they to a man than father or mother! Now that they have brought me to the verge of death, how perverse it would be of me to refuse to obey them. . . . So now I think of heaven and earth as a great furnace and the Creator as a skilled smith. What place could he send me that would not be all right? I will go off peacefully to sleep, and then with a start I will wake up."

—CHUANG-TZU

They so mean around here, they steal your sweat.

—SONNY LISTON

CHARACTERS

MARTIN

RICHIE

CARLYLE

BILLY

ROGER

COKES

ROONEY

M.P. LIEUTENANT

PFC HINSON (M.P.)

PFC CLARK (M.P.)

ACT ONE

The set is a large cadre room thrusting angularly toward the audience. The floor is wooden and brown. Brightly waxed in places, it is worn and dull in other sections. The back wall is brown and angled. There are two lights at the center of the ceiling. They hang covered by green metal shades. Against the back wall and to the stage right side are three wall lockers, side by side. Stage center in the back wall is the door, the only entrance to the room. It opens onto a hallway that runs off to the latrines, showers, other cadre rooms, and larger barracks rooms. There are three bunks. Billy's bunk is parallel to Roger's bunk. They are upstage and on either side of the room, and face downstage. Richie's bunk is downstage and at a right angle to Billy's bunk. At the foot of each bunk is a green wooden footlocker. There is a floor outlet near Roger's bunk. He uses it for his radio. A reading lamp is clamped on to the metal piping at the head of Richie's bunk. A wooden chair stands beside the wall lockers. Two mops hang in the stage-left corner near a trashcan.

It is dusk as the lights rise on the room. RICHIE is seated and bowed forward wearily on his bunk. He wears his long-sleeved khaki summer dress uniform. Upstage behind him is MARTIN, a thin, dark young man, pacing, worried. A white towel stained red with blood is wrapped around his wrist. He paces several steps and falters, stops. He stands there.

RICHIE: Honest to God, Martin, I don't know what to say anymore. I don't know what to tell you.

MARTIN (*beginning to pace again*): I mean it. I just can't stand it. Look at me.

RICHIE: I know.

MARTIN: I hate it.

RICHIE: We've got to make up a story. They'll ask you a hundred questions.

5

MARTIN: Do you know how I hate it?
RICHIE: Everybody does. Don't you think I hate it, too?
MARTIN: I enlisted, though. I enlisted and I hate it.
RICHIE: I enlisted, too.
MARTIN: I vomit every morning. I get the dry heaves. In the middle
     of every night. (*He flops down on the corner of Billy's bed and sits
     there, slumped forward, shaking his head.*)
RICHIE: You can stop that. You can.
MARTIN: No.
RICHIE: You're just scared. It's just fear.
MARTIN: They're all so mean; they're all so awful. I've got two years
     to go. Just thinking about it is going to make me sick. I thought it
     would be different from the way it is.
RICHIE: But you could have died, for God's sake. (*Turning, now he is
     facing* MARTIN.)
MARTIN: I just wanted out.
RICHIE: I might not have found you, though. I might not have come
     up here.
MARTIN: I don't care. I'd be out.

(*The door opens and a black man in filthy fatigues—they are greasestained and dark with sweat—stands there. He is* CARLYLE, *looking
about.* RICHIE, *seeing him, rises and moves toward him.*)

RICHIE: No. Roger isn't here right now.
CARLYLE: Who isn't?
RICHIE: He isn't here.
CARLYLE: They tole me a black boy livin' in here. I don't see him.
     (*He looks suspiciously about the room.*)
RICHIE: That's what I'm saying. He isn't here. He'll be back later.
     You can come back later. His name is Roger.
MARTIN: I slit my wrist. (*Thrusting out the bloody, towel-wrapped
     wrist toward* CARLYLE.)
RICHIE: Martin! Jesus!
MARTIN: I did.
RICHIE: He's kidding. He's kidding.
CARLYLE: What was his name? Martin? (*He is confused, and the*

confusion has made him angry. He moves toward MARTIN.) You
Martin?
MARTIN: Yes.

(As BILLY, *a white in his mid-twenties, blond and trim, appears in the
door, whistling, carrying a slice of pie on a paper napkin. Sensing
something, he falters, looks at* CARLYLE, *then* RICHIE.)

BILLY: Hey, what's goin' on?
CARLYLE (*turning, leaving*):Nothin', man. Not a thing.

(BILLY *looks questioningly at* RICHIE. *Then, after placing the piece of
pie on the chair beside the door, he crosses to his footlocker.*)

RICHIE: He came in looking for Roger, but he didn't even know his
name.
BILLY (*sitting on his footlocker, he starts taking off his shoes*): How come
you weren't at dinner, Rich? I brought you a piece of pie. Hey,
Martin.

(MARTIN *thrusts out his towel-wrapped wrist.*)

MARTIN: I cut my wrist, Billy.
RICHIE: Oh, for God's sake, Martin! (*He whirls away.*)
BILLY: Huh?
MARTIN: I did.
RICHIE: You are disgusting, Martin.
MARTIN: No. It's the truth. I did. I am not disgusting.
RICHIE: Well, maybe it isn't disgusting, but it certainly is disap-
pointing.
BILLY: What are you guys talking about? (*Sitting there, he really
doesn't know what is going on.*)
MARTIN: I cut my wrists, I slashed them, and Richie is pretending I
didn't.
RICHIE: I am not. And you only cut one wrist and you didn't slash it.
MARTIN: I can't stand the army anymore, Billy. (*He is moving now to
petition* BILLY, *and* RICHIE *steps between them.*)
RICHIE: Billy, listen to me. This is between Martin and me.
MARTIN: It's between me and the army, Richie.
RICHIE (*taking* MARTIN *by the shoulders as* BILLY *is now trying to*

get near MARTIN): Let's just go outside and talk, Martin. You don't know what you're saying.

BILLY: Can I see? I mean, did he really do it?

RICHIE: No!

MARTIN: I did.

BILLY: That's awful. Jesus. Maybe you should go to the infirmary.

RICHIE: I washed it with peroxide. It's not deep. Just let us be. Please. He just needs to straighten out his thinking a little, that's all.

BILLY: Well, maybe I could help him?

MARTIN: Maybe he could.

RICHIE (*suddenly pushing at* MARTIN. RICHIE *is angry and exasperated. He wants* MARTIN *out of the room*): Get out of here, Martin. Billy, you do some push-ups or something.

(*Having been pushed toward the door,* MARTIN *wanders out.*)

BILLY: No.

RICHIE: I know what Martin needs. (*Whirls and rushes into the hall after* MARTIN, *leaving* BILLY *scrambling to get his shoes on.*)

BILLY: You're no doctor, are you? I just want to make sure he doesn't have to go to the infirmary, then I'll leave you alone. (*One shoe on, he grabs up the second and runs out the door into the hall after them.*) Martin! Martin, wait up!

(*Silence. The door has been left open. Fifteen or twenty seconds pass. Then someone is heard coming down the hall. He is singing "Get a Job" and trying to do the voices and harmonies of a vocal group.* ROGER, *a tall, well-built black in long-sleeved khakis, comes in the door. He has a laundry bag over his shoulder, a pair of clean civilian trousers and a shirt on a hanger in his other hand. After dropping the bag on his bed, he goes to his wall locker, where he carefully hangs up the civilian clothes. Returning to the bed, he picks up the laundry and then, as if struck, he throws the bag down on the bed, tears off his tie, and sits down angrily on the bed. For a moment, with his head in his hands, he sits there. Then, resolutely, he rises, takes up the position of attention, and simply topples forward, his hands leaping out to break his fall at the last instant and putting him into the push-up position. Counting in a hissing, whispering voice, he does ten push-ups before*

*giving up and flopping onto his belly. He simply doesn't have the will to
do any more. Lying there, he counts rapidly on.)*

ROGER: Fourteen, fifteen. Twenty. Twenty-five.

(BILLY, *shuffling dejectedly back in, sees* ROGER *lying there.* ROGER
*springs to his feet, heads toward his footlocker, out of which he takes
an ashtray and a pack of cigarettes.)*

You come in this area, you come in here marchin', boy: standin'
tall.

(BILLY, *having gone to his wall locker, is tossing a* Playboy *magazine
onto his bunk. He will also remove a towel, a Dopp kit, and a can of
foot powder.)*

BILLY: I was marchin'.
ROGER: You call that marchin'?
BILLY: I was as tall as I am; I was marchin'—what do you want?
ROGER: Outa here, man; outa this goddamn typin'-terrors outfit and
into some kinda real army. Or else out and free.
BILLY: So go; who's stoppin' you; get out. Go on.
ROGER: Ain't you a bitch.
BILLY: You and me more regular army than the goddamn sergeants
around this place, you know that?
ROGER: I was you, Billy boy, I wouldn't be talkin' so sacrilegious so
loud, or they be doin' you like they did the ole sarge.
BILLY: He'll get off.
ROGER: Sheee-it, he'll get off.

(*Sitting down on the side of his bed and facing* BILLY, ROGER *lights up
a cigarette.* BILLY *has arranged the towel, Dopp kit and foot powder on
his own bed.)*

Don't you think L.B.J. want to have some sergeants in that
Vietnam, man? In Disneyland, baby? Lord have mercy on the ole
sarge. He goin' over there to be Mickey Mouse.

BILLY: Do him a lot of good. Make a man outa him.
ROGER: That's right, that's right. He said the same damn thing
about himself and you, too, I do believe. You know what's the ole

boy's MOS? His Military Occupation Specialty? Demolitions, baby. Expert is his name.

BILLY (*taking off his shoes and beginning to work on a sore toe, he hardly looks up*): You're kiddin' me.

ROGER: Do I jive?

BILLY: You mean that poor ole bastard who cannot light his own cigar for shakin' is supposed to go over there blowin' up bridges and shit? Do they wanna win this war or not, man?

ROGER: Ole sarge was over in Europe in the big one, Billy. Did all kinds a bad things.

BILLY (*swinging his feet up onto the bed, he sits, cutting the cuticles on his toes, powdering his feet*): Was he drinkin' since he got the word?

ROGER: Was he breathin', Billy? Was he breathin'?

BILLY: Well, at least he ain't cuttin' his fuckin' wrists.

(*Silence.* ROGER *looks at* BILLY, *who keeps on working.*)

Man, that's the real damn army over there, ain't it? That ain't shinin' your belt buckle and standin' tall. And we might end up in it, man.

(*Silence.* ROGER, *rising, begins to sort his laundry.*)

Roger . . . you ever ask yourself if you'd rather fight in a war where it was freezin' cold or one where there was awful snakes? You ever ask that question?

ROGER: Can't say I ever did.

BILLY: We used to ask it all the time. All the time. I mean, us kids sittin' out on the back porch tellin' ghost stories at night. 'Cause it was Korea time and the newspapers were fulla pictures of soldiers in snow with white frozen beards; they got these rags tied around their feet. And snakes. We hated snakes. Hated 'em. I mean, it's bad enough to be in the jungle duckin' bullets, but then you crawl right into a goddamn snake. That's awful. That's awful.

ROGER: It don't sound none too good.

BILLY: I got my draft notice, goddamn Vietnam didn't even exist. I mean, it existed, but not as in a war we might be in. I started crawlin' around the floor a this house where I was stayin' 'cause I'd dropped outa school, and I was goin' "Bang, bang," pretendin'. Jesus.

ROGER (*continuing with his laundry, he tries to joke*): My first goddamn formation in basic, Billy, this NCO's up there jammin' away about how some a us are goin' to be dyin' in the war. I'm sayin', "What war? What that crazy man talkin' about?"

BILLY: Us, too. I couldn't believe it. I couldn't believe it. And now we got three people goin' from here.

ROGER: Five.

(*They look at each other, and then turn away, each returning to his task.*)

BILLY: It don't seem possible. I mean, people shootin' at you. Shootin' at you to kill you. (*Slight pause.*) It's somethin'.

ROGER: What did you decide you preferred?

BILLY: Huh?

ROGER: Did you decide you would prefer the snakes or would you prefer the snow? 'Cause it look like it is going to be the snakes.

BILLY: I think I had pretty much made my mind up on the snow.

ROGER: Well, you just let 'em know that, Billy. Maybe they get one goin' special just for you up in Alaska. You can go to the Klondike. Fightin' some snowmen.

(RICHIE *bounds into the room and shuts the door as if to keep out something dreadful. He looks at* ROGER *and* BILLY *and crosses to his wall locker, pulling off his tie as he moves. Tossing the tie into the locker, he begins unbuttoning the cuffs of his shirt.*)

RICHIE: Hi, hi, hi, everybody. Billy, hello.

BILLY: Hey.

ROGER: What's happenin', Rich?

(*Moving to the chair beside the door,* RICHIE *picks up the pie* BILLY *left there. He will place the pie atop the locker, and then, sitting, he will remove his shoes and socks.*)

RICHIE: I simply did this rather wonderful thing for a friend of mine, helped him see himself in a clearer, more hopeful light—

a little room in his life for hope. And I feel very good. Didn't Billy
tell you?

ROGER: About what?

RICHIE: About Martin.

ROGER: No.

BILLY (*looking up and speaking pointedly*): No.

(RICHIE *looks at* BILLY *and then at* ROGER. RICHIE *is truly confused.*)

RICHIE: No? No?

BILLY: What do I wanna gossip about Martin for?

RICHIE (*really can't figure out what is going on with* BILLY; *shoes and socks in hand, he heads for his wall locker*): Who was planning to gossip? I mean, it did happen. We could talk about it. I mean, I wasn't hearing his goddamn confession. Oh, my sister told me Catholics were boring.

BILLY: Good thing I ain't one anymore.

RICHIE (*taking off his shirt, moves toward* ROGER): It really wasn't anything, Roger, except Martin made this rather desperate, pathetic gesture for attention that seems to have brought to the surface Billy's more humane and protective side. (*Reaching out, he tousles Billy's hair.*)

BILLY: Man, I am gonna have to obliterate you.

RICHIE (*tossing his shirt into his locker*): I don't know what you're so embarrassed about.

BILLY: I just think Martin's got enough trouble without me yappin' to everybody.

(RICHIE *has moved nearer* BILLY, *his manner playful and teasing.*)

RICHIE: "Obliterate"? "Obliterate," did you say? Oh, Billy, you better say "shit," "ain't," and "motherfucker" real quick now, or we'll all know just how far beyond the fourth grade you went.

ROGER (*having moved to his locker, into which he is placing his folded clothes*): You hear about the ole sarge, Richard?

BILLY (*grinning*): You ain't . . . shit . . . motherfucker.

ROGER (*laughing*): All right.

RICHIE (*moving center and beginning to remove his trousers*): Billy, no, no. Wit is my domain. You're in charge of sweat and running around the block.

ROGER: You hear about the ole sarge?

RICHIE: What about the ole sarge? Oh, who cares? Let's go to a movie. Billy, wanna? Let's go. C'mon. (*Trousers off, he hurries to his locker.*)

BILLY: Sure. What's playin'?

RICHIE: I don't know. Can't remember. Something good, though.

(*With a* Playboy *magazine he has taken from his locker,* ROGER *is settling down on his bunk, his back toward both* BILLY *and* RICHIE.)

BILLY: You wanna go, Rog?

RICHIE (*in mock irritation*): Don't ask Roger! How are we going to kiss and hug and stuff if he's there?

BILLY: That ain't funny, man. (*He is stretched out on his bunk, and* RICHIE *comes bounding over to flop down and lie beside him.*)

RICHIE: And what time will you pick me up?

BILLY (*pushes at* RICHIE, *knocking him off the bed and onto the floor*): Well, you just fall down and wait, all right?

RICHIE: Can I help it if I love you? (*Leaping to his feet, he will head to his locker, remove his shorts, put on a robe.*)

ROGER: You gonna take a shower, Richard?

RICHIE: Cleanliness is nakedness, Roger.

ROGER: Is that right? I didn't know that. Not too many people know that. You may be the only person in the world who know that.

RICHIE: And godliness is in there somewhere, of course. (*Putting a towel around his neck, he is gathering toiletries to carry to the shower.*)

ROGER: You got your own way a lookin' at things, man. You cute.

RICHIE: That's right.

ROGER: You g'wan, have a good time in that shower.

RICHIE: Oh, I will.

BILLY (*without looking up from his feet, which he is powdering*): And don't drop your soap.

RICHIE: I will if I want to. (*Already out the door, he slams it shut with a flourish.*)

BILLY: Can you imagine bein' in combat with Richie—people blastin' away at you—he'd probably want to hold your hand.

ROGER: Ain't he somethin'?

BILLY: Who's zat?

ROGER: He's all right.

BILLY (*rising, heading toward his wall locker, where he will put the powder and Dopp kit*): Sure he is, except he's livin' under water.

(*Looking at* BILLY, ROGER *senses something unnerving; it makes* ROGER *rise, and return his magazine to his footlocker.*)

ROGER: I think we oughta do this area, man. I think we oughta do our area. Mop and buff this floor.

BILLY: You really don't think he means that shit he talks, do you?

ROGER: Huh? Awwww, man . . . Billy, no.

BILLY: I'd put money on it, Roger, and I ain't got much money.

(BILLY *is trying to face* ROGER *with this, but* ROGER, *seated on his bed, has turned away. He is unbuttoning his shirt.*)

ROGER: Man, no, no. I'm tellin' you, lad, you listen to the ole Rog. You seen that picture a that little dolly he's got in his locker? He ain't swish, man, believe me—he's cool.

BILLY: It's just that ever since we been in this room, he's been different somehow. Somethin'.

ROGER: No, he ain't.

(BILLY *turns to his bed, where he carefully starts folding the towel. Then he looks at* ROGER.)

BILLY: You ever talk to any a these guys—queers, I mean? You ever sit down, just rap with one of 'em?

ROGER: Hell, no; what I wanna do that for? Shit, no.

BILLY (*crossing to the trash can in the corner, where he will shake the towel empty*): I mean, some of 'em are okay guys, just way up this bad alley, and you say to 'em, "I'm straight, be cool," they go their own way. But then there's these other ones, these bitches, man, and they're so crazy they think anybody can be had. Because they been had themselves. So you tell 'em you're straight and they just nod and smile. You ain't real to 'em. They can't see nothin' but themselves and these goddamn games they're always playin'. (*Having returned to his bunk, he is putting on his shoes.*) I mean, you can be decent about anything, Roger, you see what I'm sayin'? We're all just people, man, and some of us are hardly that. That's all I'm sayin'. (*There is a slight pause as he sits there thinking. Then he gets to his feet.*) I'll go get some buckets and stuff so we can clean up, okay? This area's a mess. This area ain't standin' tall.

ROGER: That's good talk, lad; this area a midget you put it next to an area standin' tall.

BILLY: Got to be good fuckin' troopers.

ROGER: That's right, that's right. I know the meanin' of the words.

BILLY: I mean, I just think we all got to be honest with each other— you understand me?

ROGER: No, I don't understand you; one stupid fuckin' nigger like me—how's that gonna be?

BILLY: That's right; mock me, man. That's what I need. I'll go get the wax.

(*Out* BILLY *goes, talking to himself and leaving the door open. For a moment* ROGER *sits, thinking, and then he looks at Richie's locker and gets to his feet and walks to the locker which he opens and looks at the pinup hanging on the inside of the door. He takes a step backward, looking.*)

ROGER: Sheee-it.

(*Through the open door comes* CARLYLE. ROGER *doesn't see him. And* CARLYLE *stands there looking at* ROGER *and the picture in the locker.*)

CARLYLE: Boy . . . whose locker you lookin' into?

ROGER (*startled, but recovers*): Hey, baby, what's happenin'?

CARLYLE: That ain't your locker, is what I'm askin', nigger. I mean, you ain't got no white goddamn woman hangin' on your wall.

ROGER: Oh, no—no, no.

CARLYLE: You don't wanna be lyin' to me, 'cause I got to turn you in you lyin' and you do got the body a some white goddamn woman hangin' there for you to peek at nobody around but you—you can be thinkin' about that sweet wet pussy an' maybe it hot an' maybe it cool.

ROGER: I could be thinkin' all that, except I know the penalty for lyin'.

CARLYLE: Thank God for that.

(*Extending his hand, palm up*)

ROGER: That's right. This here the locker of a faggot. (*And he slaps Carlyle's hand, palm to palm.*)
CARLYLE: Course it is; I see that; any damn body know that.

(ROGER *crosses toward his bunk and* CARLYLE *swaggers about, pulling a pint of whiskey from his hip pocket.*)

You want a shot? Have you a little taste, my man.

ROGER: Naw.
CARLYLE: C'mon. C'mon. I think you a Tom you don't drink outa my bottle.

(*He thrusts the bottle toward* ROGER *and wipes a sweat-and greasestained sleeve across his mouth.*)

ROGER (*taking the bottle*): Shit.
CARLYLE: That right. How do I know? I just got in. New boy in town. Somewhere over there; I dunno. They dump me in amongst a whole bunch a pale, boring motherfuckers. (*He is exploring the room. Finding Billy's* Playboy, *he edges onto Billy's bed and leafs nervously through the pages.*) I just come in from P Company, man, and I been all over this place, don't see too damn many of us. This outfit look like it a little short on soul. I been walkin' all around, I tell you, and the number is small. Like one hand you can tabulate the lot of 'em. We got few brothers I been able to see, is what I'm sayin'. You and me and two cats down in the small bay. That's all I found.

(*As* ROGER *is about to hand the bottle back,* CARLYLE, *almost angrily, waves him off.*)

No, no, you take another; take you a real taste.

ROGER: It ain't so bad here. We do all right.
CARLYLE (*moves, shutting the door; suspiciously, he approaches* ROGER): How about the white guys? They give you any sweat? What's the situation? No jive. I like to know what is goin' on within the situation before that situation get a chance to be closin' in on me.

ROGER (*putting the bottle on the footlocker, he sits down*): Man, I'm tellin' you, it ain't bad. They're just pale, most of 'em, you know. They can't help it; how they gonna help it? Some of 'em got little bit a soul, couple real good boys around this way. Get 'em little bit of Coppertone, they be straight, man.

CARLYLE: How about the NCOs? We got any brother NCO watchin' out for us or they all white, like I goddamn well KNOW all the officers are? Fuckin' officers always white, man; fuckin' snow cones and bars everywhere you look. (*He cannot stay still. He moves to his right, his left; he sits, he stands.*)

ROGER: First sergeant's a black man.

CARLYLE: All right; good news. Hey, hey, you wanna go over the club with me, or maybe downtown? I got wheels. Let's be free. (*Now he rushes at* ROGER.) Let's be free.

ROGER: Naw . . .

CARLYLE: Ohhh, baby . . . !

(*He is pulling wildly at* ROGER *to get him to the door.*)

ROGER: Some other time. I gotta get the area straight. Me and the guy sleeps in here too are gonna shape the place up a little. (*He has pulled free, and* CARLYLE *cannot understand. It hurts him, depresses him.*)

CARLYLE: You got a sweet deal here an' you wanna keep it, that right? (*He paces about the room, opens a footlocker, looks inside.*) How you rate you get a room like this for yourself—you and a couple guys?

ROGER: Spec 4. The three of us in here Spec 4.

CARLYLE: You get a room then, huh? (*And suddenly, without warning or transition, he is angry.*) Oh, man, I hate this goddamn army. I hate this bastard army. I mean, I just got outa basic—off leave— you know? Back on the block for two weeks—and now here. They don't pull any a that petty shit, now, do they—that god- damn petty basic training bullshit? They do and I'm gonna be bustin' some head—my hand is gonna be upside all kinds a heads, 'cause I ain't gonna be able to endure it, man, not that kinda crap—understand? (*And again, he is rushing at* ROGER.) Hey, hey, oh, c'mon, let's get my wheels and make it, man, do me the favor.

ROGER: How'm I gonna? I got my obligations.

(*And* CARLYLE *spins away in anger.*)

CARLYLE: Jesus, baby, can't you remember the outside? How long it been since you been on leave? It is so sweet out there, nigger; you got it all forgot. I had such a sweet, sweet time. They doin' dances, baby, make you wanna cry. I hate this damn army. (*The anger overwhelms him.*) All these mother-actin' jacks givin' you jive about what you gotta do and what you can't do. I had a bad scene in basic—up the hill and down the hill; it ain't somethin' I enjoyed even a little. So they do me wrong here, Jim, they gonna be sorry. Some-damn-body! And this whole Vietnam THING—I do not dig it. (*He falls on his knees before* ROGER. *It is a gesture that begins as a joke, a mockery. And then a real fear pulses through him to nearly fill the pose he has taken.*) Lord, Lord, don't let 'em touch me. Christ, what will I do, they DO! Whooooooooooooo! And they pullin' guys outa here, too, ain't they? Pullin' 'em like weeds, man; throwin' 'em into the fire. It's shit, man.

ROGER: They got this ole sarge sleeps down the hall—just today they got him.

CARLYLE: Which ole sarge?

ROGER: He sleeps just down the hall. Little guy.

CARLYLE: Wino, right?

ROGER: Booze hound.

CARLYLE: Yeh; I seen him. They got him, huh?

ROGER: He's goin'; gotta be packin' his bags. And three other guys two days ago. And two guys last week.

CARLYLE (*leaping up from Billy's bed*): Ohhh, them bastards. And everybody just takes it. It ain't our war, brother. I'm tellin' you. That's what gets me, nigger. It ain't our war nohow because it ain't our country, and that's what burns my ass—that and everybody just sittin' and takin' it. They gonna be bustin' balls, man— kickin' and stompin'. Everybody here maybe one week from shippin' out to get blown clean away and, man, whata they doin'? They doin' what they told. That what they doin'. Like you? Shit! You gonna straighten up your goddamn area! Well, that ain't for me; I'm gettin' hat, and makin' it out where it's sweet and the people's livin'. I can't cut this jive here, man. I'm tellin' you. I can't cut it.

(*He has moved toward* ROGER, *and behind him now* RICHIE *enters, running, his hair wet, traces of shaving cream on his face. Toweling his hair, he falters, seeing* CARLYLE. *Then he crosses to his locker.* CARLYLE *grins at* ROGER, *looks at* RICHIE, *steps toward him and gives a little bow.*)

My name is Carlyle; what is yours?

RICHIE: Richie.

CARLYLE (*turns toward* ROGER *to share his joke*): Hello. Where is Martin? That cute little Martin.

(*And* RICHIE *has just taken off his robe as* CARLYLE *turns back.*)

You cute, too, Richie.

RICHIE: Martin doesn't live here. (*Hurriedly putting on underpants to cover his nakedness*)

CARLYLE (*watching* RICHIE, *he slowly turns toward* ROGER): You ain't gonna make it with me, man?

ROGER: Naw . . . like I tole you. I'll catch you later.

CARLYLE: That's sad, man; make me cry in my heart.

ROGER: You g'wan get your head smokin'. Stop on back.

CARLYLE: Okay, okay. Got to be one man one more time. (*On the move for the door, his hand extended palm up behind him, demanding the appropriate response.*) Baby! Gimme! Gimme!

(*Lunging,* ROGER *slaps the hand.*)

ROGER: G'wan home! G'wan home.

CARLYLE: You gonna hear from me. (*And he is gone out the door and down the hallway.*)

ROGER: I can . . . and do . . . believe . . . that.

(RICHIE, *putting on his T-shirt, watches* ROGER, *who stubs out his cigarette, then crosses to the trashcan to empty the ashtray.*)

RICHIE: Who was that?

ROGER: Man's new, Rich. Dunno his name more than that "Carlyle" he said. He's new—just outa basic.

RICHIE (*powdering his thighs and under his arms*): Oh, my God . . .

(*As* BILLY *enters, pushing a mop bucket with a wringer attached and carrying a container of wax.*)

ROGER: Me and Billy's gonna straighten up the area. You wanna help?

RICHIE: Sure, sure; help, help.

BILLY (*talking to* ROGER, *but turning to look at* RICHIE, *who is still putting powder under his arms*): I hadda steal the wax from Third Platoon.

ROGER: Good man.

BILLY (*moving to* RICHIE, *joking, yet really irritated in some strange way*): What? Whata you doin', singin'? Look at that, Rog. He's got enough jazz there for an entire beauty parlor. (*Grabbing the can from* RICHIE'S *hand.*) What is this? Baby Powder! BABY POWDER!

RICHIE: I get rashes.

BILLY: Okay, okay, you get rashes, so what? They got powder for rashes that isn't baby powder.

RICHIE: It doesn't work as good; I've tried it. Have you tried it?

(*Grabbing Billy's waist,* RICHIE *pulls him close.* BILLY *knocks Richie's hands away.*)

BILLY: Man, I wish you could get yourself straight. I'll mop, too, Roger—okay? Then I'll put down the wax and you can spread it? (*He has walked away from* RICHIE.)

RICHIE: What about buffing?

ROGER: In the morning. (*He is already busy mopping up near the door.*)

RICHIE: What do you want me to do?

BILLY (*grabbing up a mop, he heads downstage to work*): Get inside your locker and shut the door and don't holler for help. Nobody'll know you're there; you'll stay there.

RICHIE: But I'm so pretty.

BILLY: NOW! (*Pointing to* ROGER. *He wants to get this clear.*) Tell that man you mean what you're sayin', Richie.

RICHIE: Mean what?

BILLY: That you really think you're pretty.

RICHIE: Of course I do; I am. Don't you think I am? Don't you think I am, Roger?

ROGER: I tole you—you fulla shit and you cute, man. Carlyle just tole you you cute, too.

RICHIE: Don't you think it's true, Billy?

BILLY: It's like I tole you, Rog.

RICHIE: What did you tell him?

BILLY: That you go down; that you go up and down like a yo-yo and you go blowin' all the trees like the wind.

(RICHIE *is stunned. He looks at* ROGER, *and then he turns and stares into his own locker. The others keep mopping.* RICHIE *takes out a towel, and putting it around his neck, he walks to where* BILLY *is working. He stands there, hurt, looking at* BILLY.)

RICHIE: What the hell made you tell him I been down, Billy?

BILLY (*still mopping*): It's in your eyes; I seen it.

RICHIE: What?

BILLY: You.

RICHIE: What is it, Billy, you think you're trying to say? You and all your wit and intelligence—your HUMANITY.

BILLY: I said it, Rich; I said what I was tryin' to say.

RICHIE: DID you?

BILLY: I think I did.

RICHIE: DO you?

BILLY: Loud and clear, baby. (*Still mopping.*)

ROGER: They got to put me in with the weirdos. Why is that, huh? How come the army HATE me, do this shit to me—KNOW what to do to me. (*Whimsical, and then suddenly loud, angered, violent.*) Now you guys put socks in your mouths, right now—get shut up—or I am gonna beat you to death with each other. Roger got work to do. To be doin' it!

RICHIE (*turning to his bed, he kneels upon it*): Roger, I think you're so innocent sometimes. Honestly, it's not such a terrible thing. Is it, Billy?

BILLY: How would I know? (*He slams his mop into the bucket.*) Oh, go fuck yourself.

RICHIE: Well, I can give it a try, if that's what you want. Can I think of you as I do?

BILLY (*throwing down his mop*): GODDAMMIT! That's it! IT!

(BILLY *exits, rushing into the hall and slamming the door behind him.* ROGER *looks at* RICHIE. *Neither quite knows what is going on. Suddenly the door bursts open and* BILLY *storms straight over to* RICHIE, *who still kneels on the bed.*)

Now I am gonna level with you. Are you gonna listen? You gonna hear what I say, Rich, and not what you think I'm sayin'?

(RICHIE *turns away as if to rise, his manner flippant, disdainful.*)

No! Don't get cute; don't turn away cute. I wanna say somethin' straight out to you and I want you to hear it!

RICHIE: I'm all ears, goddammit! For what, however, I do not know, except some boring evasion.

BILLY: At least wait the hell till you hear me!

RICHIE (*in irritation*): Okay, okay! What?

BILLY: Now this is level, Rich; this is straight talk. (*He is quiet, intense. This is difficult for him. He seeks the exactly appropriate words of explanation.*) No B.S. No tricks. What you do on the side, that's your business and I don't care about it. But if you don't cut the cute shit with me, I'm gonna turn you off. Completely. You ain't gonna get a good mornin' outa me, you understand, because it's gettin' bad around here. I mean, I know how you think—how you keep lookin' out and seein' yourself, and that's what I'm tryin' to tell you because that's all that's happenin', Rich. That's all there is to it when you look out at me and think there's some kind of approval or whatever you see in my eyes—you're just seein' yourself. And I'm talkin' the simple quiet truth to you, Rich. I swear I am.

(BILLY *looks away from* RICHIE *now and tries to go back to the mopping. It is embarrassing for them all.* ROGER *has watched, has tried to keep working.* RICHIE *has flopped back on his bunk. There is a silence.*)

RICHIE: How . . . do . . . you want me to be? I don't know how else to be.

BILLY: Ohhh, man, that ain't any part of it. (*The mop is clenched in his hands.*)

RICHIE: Well, I don't come from the same kind of world as you do.

BILLY: Damn, Richie, you think Roger and I come off the same street?

ROGER: Shit . . .

RICHIE: All right. Okay. But I've just done what I wanted all of my life. If I wanted to do something, I just did it. Honestly. I've never had to work or anything like that, and I've always had nice clothing and money for cab fare. Money for whatever I wanted. Always. I'm not like you are.

ROGER: You ain't sayin' you really done that stuff, though, Rich.

RICHIE: What?

ROGER: That fag stuff.

RICHIE (*continues looking at* ROGER *and then he looks away*): Yes.

ROGER: Do you even know what you're sayin', Richie? Do you even know what it means to be a fag?

RICHIE: Roger, of course I know what it is. I just told you I've done it. I thought you black people were supposed to understand all about suffering and human strangeness. I thought you had depth and vision from all your suffering. Has someone been misleading me? I just told you I did it. I know all about it. Everything. All the various positions.

ROGER: Yeh, so maybe you think you've tried it, but that don't make you it. I mean, we used to . . . in the old neighborhood, man, we had a couple dudes swung that way. But they was weird, man. There was this one little fella, he was a screamin' goddamn faggot . . . uh . . . (*He considers* RICHIE, *wondering if perhaps he has offended him.*) Ohhh, ohhh, you ain't no screamin' goddamn faggot, Richie, no matter what you say. And the baddest man on the block was my boy Jerry Lemon. So one day Jerry's got the faggot in one a them ole deserted stairways and he's bouncin' him off the walls. I'm just a little fella, see, and I'm watchin' the baddest man on the block do his thing. So he come bouncin' back into me instead of Jerry, and just when he hit, he gave his ass this little twitch, man, like he thought he was gonna turn me on. I'd never a thought that was possible, man, for a man to be twitchin' his ass on me, just like he thought he was a broad. Scared me to death. I took off runnin'. Oh, oh, that ole neighborhood put me into all kinds a crap. I did some sufferin', just like Richie says.

Like this once, I'm swingin' on up the street after school, and
outa this phone booth comes this man with a goddamned knife
stickin' outa his gut. So he sees me and starts tryin' to pull his
motherfuckin' coat out over the handle, like he's worried about
how he looks, man. "I didn't know this was gonna happen," he
says. And then he falls over. He was just all of a sudden dead,
man; just all of a sudden dead. You ever seen anything like that,
Billy? Any crap like that?

(BILLY, *sitting on Roger's bunk, is staring at* ROGER.)

BILLY: You really seen that?
ROGER: Richie's a big-city boy.
RICHIE: Oh, no; never anything like that.
ROGER: "Momma, help me," I am screamin'. "Jesus, Momma, help
me." Little fella, he don't know how to act, he sees somethin' like
that.

(*For a moment they are still, each thinking.*)

BILLY: How long you think we got?
ROGER: What do you mean?

(ROGER *is hanging up the mops;* BILLY *is now kneeling on Roger's
bunk.*)

BILLY: Till they pack us up, man, ship us out.
ROGER: To the war, you mean? To Disneyland? Man, I dunno; that
up to them IBMs. Them machines is figurin' that. Maybe tomorrow, maybe next week, maybe never.

(*The war—the threat of it—is the one thing they share.*)

RICHIE: I was reading they're planning to build it all up to more
than five hundred thousand men over there. Americans. And
they're going to keep it that way until they win.
BILLY: Be a great place to come back from, man, you know? I keep
thinkin' about that. To have gone there, to have been there, to
have seen it and lived.
ROGER (*settling onto Billy's bunk, lights a cigarette*): Well, what we
got right here is a fool, gonna probably be one a them five
hundred thousand, too. Do you know I cry at the goddamn

anthem yet sometimes? The flag is flyin' at a ball game, the ole Roger gets all wet in the eye. After all the shit been done to his black ass. But I don't know what I think about this war. I do not know.

BILLY: I'm tellin' you, Rog—I've been doin' a lot a readin' and I think it's right we go. I mean, it's just like when North Korea invaded South Korea or when Hitler invaded Poland and all those other countries. He just kept testin' everybody and when nobody said no to him, he got so committed he couldn't back out even if he wanted. And that's what this Ho Chi Minh is doin'. And all these other Communists. If we let 'em know somebody is gonna stand up against 'em, they'll back off, just like Hitler would have.

ROGER: There is folks, you know, who are sayin' L.B.J. is the Hitler, and not ole Ho Chi Minh at all.

RICHIE (*talking as if this is the best news he's heard in years*): Well, I don't know anything at all about all that, but I am certain I don't want to go—whatever is going on. I mean, those Vietcong don't just shoot you and blow you up, you know. My God, they've got these other awful things they do: putting elephant shit on these stakes in the ground and then you step on 'em and you got elephant shit in a wound in your foot. The infection is horrendous. And then there's these caves they hide in and when you go in after 'em, they've got these snakes that they've tied by their tails to the ceiling. So it's dark and the snake is furious from having been hung by its tail and you crawl right into them—your face. My God.

BILLY: They do not. (*Knows he has been caught; they all know it.*)

RICHIE: I read it, Billy. They do.

BILLY (*completely facetious, yet the fear is real*): That's bullshit, Richie.

ROGER: That's right, Richie. They maybe do that stuff with the elephant shit, but nobody's gonna tie a snake by its tail, let ole Billy walk into it.

BILLY: That's disgusting, man.

ROGER: Guess you better get ready for the Klondike, my man.

BILLY: That is probably the most disgusting thing I ever heard of. I DO NOT WANT TO GO! NOT TO NOWHERE WHERE

THAT KINDA SHIT IS GOIN' ON! L.B.J. is Hitler; suddenly
I see it all very clearly.

ROGER: Billy got him a hatred for snakes.

RICHIE: I hate them, too. They're hideous.

BILLY (*as a kind of apology to* RICHIE, *continues his self-ridicule far into the extreme*): I mean, that is one of the most awful things I ever heard of any person doing. I mean, any person who would hang a snake by its tail in the dark of a cave in the hope that some other person might crawl into it and get bitten to death, that first person is somebody who oughta be shot. And I hope the five hundred thousand other guys that get sent over there kill 'em all—all them gooks—get 'em all driven back into Germany, where they belong. And in the meantime, I'll be holding the northern border against the snowmen.

ROGER (*rising from Billy's bed*): And in the meantime, before that, we better be gettin' at the ole area here. Got to be strike troopers.

BILLY: Right.

RICHIE: Can I help?

ROGER: Sure. Be good. (*And he crosses to his footlocker and takes out a radio.*) Think maybe I put on a little music, though it's gettin' late. We got time. Billy, you think?

BILLY: Sure. (*Getting nervously to his feet.*)

ROGER: Sure. All right. We can be doin' it to the music. (*He plugs the radio into the floor outlet as* BILLY *bolts for the door.*)

BILLY: I gotta go pee.

ROGER: You watch out for the snakes.

BILLY: It's the snowmen, man; the snowmen.

(BILLY *is gone and "Ruby," sung by Ray Charles, comes from the radio. For a moment, as the music plays,* ROGER *watches* RICHIE *wander about the room, pouring little splashes of wax onto the floor. Then* RICHIE *moves to his bed and lies down, and* ROGER, *shaking his head, starts leisurely to spread the wax, with* RICHIE *watching.*)

RICHIE: How come you and Billy take all this so seriously—you know.

ROGER: What?

RICHIE: This army nonsense. You're always shining your brass and keeping your footlocker neat and your locker so neat. There's no point to any of it.

ROGER: We here, ain't we, Richie? We in the army. (*Still working the wax.*)

RICHIE: There's no point to any of it. And doing those push-ups, the two of you.

ROGER: We just see a lot of things the same way is all. Army ought to be a serious business, even if sometimes it ain't.

RICHIE: You're lucky, you know, the two of you. Having each other for friends the way you do. I never had that kind of friend ever. Not even when I was little.

ROGER (*after a pause during which he, while working, sort of peeks at* RICHIE *every now and then*): You ain't really inta that stuff, are you, Richie? (*It is a question that is a statement.*)

RICHIE (*coyly looks at* ROGER): What stuff is that, Roger?

ROGER: That fag stuff, man. You know. You ain't really into it, are you? You maybe messed in it a little is all—am I right?

RICHIE: I'm very weak, Roger. And by that I simply mean that if I have an impulse to do something, I don't know how to deny myself. If I feel like doing something, I just do it. I . . . will . . . admit to sometimes wishin' I . . . was a little more like you . . . and Billy, even, but not to any severe extent.

ROGER: But that's such a bad scene, Rich. You don't want that. Nobody wants that. Nobody wants to be a punk. Not nobody. You wanna know what I think it is? You just got in with the wrong bunch. Am I right? You just got in with a bad bunch. That can happen. And that's what I think happened to you. I bet you never had a chance to really run with the boys before. I mean, regular normal guys like Billy and me. How'd you come in the army, huh, Richie? You get drafted?

RICHIE: No.

ROGER: That's my point, see. (*He has stopped working. He stands, leaning on the mop, looking at* RICHIE.)

RICHIE: About four years ago, I went to this party. I was very young, and I went to this party with a friend who was older and . . . this "fag stuff," as you call it, was going on . . . so I did it.

ROGER: And then you come in the army to get away from it, right? Huh?

RICHIE: I don't know.

ROGER: Sure.

RICHIE: I don't know, Roger.

ROGER: Sure; sure. And now you're gettin' a chance to run with the boys for a little, you'll get yourself straightened around. I know it for a fact; I know that thing.

(*From off there is the sudden loud bellowing sound of* SERGEANT ROONEY.)

ROONEY: THERE AIN'T BEEN NO SOLDIERS IN THIS CAMP BUT ME. I BEEN THE ONLY ONE—I BEEN THE ONLY ME!

(*And* BILLY *comes dashing into the room.*)

BILLY: Oh, boy.

ROGER: Guess who?

ROONEY: FOR SO LONG I BEEN THE ONLY GODDAMN ONE!

BILLY (*leaping onto his bed and covering his face with a* Playboy *magazine as* RICHIE *is trying to disappear under his sheets and blankets and* ROGER *is trying to get the wax put away so he can get into his own bunk*): Hut who hee whor—he's got some yo-yo with him, Rog!

ROGER: Huh?

(*As* COKES *and* ROONEY *enter. Both are in fatigues and drunk and big-bellied. They are in their fifties, their hair whitish and cut short. Both men carry whiskey bottles, beer bottles.* COKES *is a little neater than* ROONEY, *his fatigue jacket tucked in and not so rumpled, and he wears canvas-sided jungle boots.* ROONEY, *very disheveled, chomps on the stub of a big cigar. They swagger in, looking for fun, and stand there side by side.*)

ROONEY: What kinda platoon I got here? You buncha shit sacks. Everybody look sharp.

(*The three boys lie there, unmoving.*)

Off and on!

COKES: OFF AND ON! (*He seems barely conscious, wavering as he stands.*)

ROGER: What's happenin', Sergeant?

ROONEY (*shoving his bottle of whiskey at* ROGER, *who is sitting up*): Shut up, Moore! You want a belt? (*Splashing whiskey on Roger's chest.*)

ROGER: How can I say no?

COKES: My name is Cokes!

BILLY (*rising to sit on the side of his bed*): How about me, too?

COKES: You wait your turn.

ROONEY (*looks at the three of them as if they are fools. Indicates* COKES *with a gesture*): Don't you see what I got here?

BILLY: Who do I follow for my turn?

ROONEY (*suddenly, crazily petulant*): Don't you see what I got here? Everybody on their feet and at attention!

(BILLY *and* ROGER *climb from their bunks and stand at attention. They don't know what* ROONEY *is mad at.*)

I mean it!

(RICHIE *bounds to the position of attention.*)

This here is my friend, who in addition just come back from the war! The goddamn war! He been to it and he come back.

(ROONEY *is patting* COKES *gently, proudly.*)

The man's a fuckin' hero!

(ROONEY *hugs* COKES, *almost kissing him on the cheek.*)

He's always been a fuckin' hero.

(COKES, *embarrassed in his stupor, kind of wobbles a little from side to side.*)

COKES: No-o-o-o-o-o . . .

(*And* ROONEY *grabs him, starts pushing him toward Billy's foot-locker.*)

ROONEY: Show 'em your boots, Cokes. Show 'em your jungle boots.

(*With a long, clumsy step,* COKES *climbs onto the footlocker,* ROONEY *supporting him from behind and then bending to lift one of* Cokes's *booted feet and display it for the boys.*)

Lookee that boot. That ain't no everyday goddamn army boot. That is a goddamn jungle boot! That green canvas is a jungle boot 'cause a the heat, and them little holes in the bottom are so the water can run out when you been walkin' in a lotta water like in a jungle swamp. (*He is extremely proud of all this; he looks at them.*) The army ain't no goddamn fool. You see a man wearin' boots like that, you might as well see he's got a chestful a medals, 'cause he been to the war. He don't have no boots like that unless he been to the war! Which is where I'm goin' and all you slaphappy mother-fuckers, too. Got to go kill some gooks. (*He is nodding at them, smiling.*) That's right.

COKES (*bursting loudly from his stupor*): Gonna piss on 'em. Old booze. 'At's what I did. Piss in the rivers. Goddamn GI's secret weapon is old booze and he's pissin' it in all their runnin' water. Makes 'em yellow. Ahhhha ha, ha, ha! (*He laughs and laughs, and* ROONEY *laughs, too, hugging* COKES.)

ROONEY: Me and Cokesy been in so much shit together we oughta be brown. (*And then he catches himself, looks at* ROGER.) Don't take no offense at that, Moore. We been swimmin' in it. One Hundred and First Airborne, together. One-oh-one. Screamin' goddamn Eagles!

(*Looking at each other, face to face, eyes glinting, they make sudden loud screaming-eagle sounds.*)

This ain't the army; you punks ain't in the army. You ain't ever seen the army. The army is Airborne! Airborne!

COKES (*beginning to stomp his feet*): Airborne, Airborne! ALL THE WAY!

(*As* RICHIE, *amused and hoping for a drink, too, reaches out toward* ROONEY.)

RICHIE: Sergeant, Sergeant, I can have a little drink, too.

(ROONEY *looks at him and clutches the bottle.*)

ROONEY: Are you kiddin' me? You gotta be kiddin' me. (*He looks to* ROGER.) He's kiddin' me, ain't he, Moore? (*And then to* BILLY *and then to* COKES.) Ain't he, Cokesy? (COKES *steps forward and down with a thump, taking charge for his bewildered friend.*)

COKES: Don't you know you are tryin' to take the booze from the hand a the future goddamn Congressional Honor winner . . . Medal . . . ? (*And he looks lovingly at* ROONEY. *He beams.*) Ole Rooney, Ole Rooney. (*He hugs Rooney's head.*) He almost done it already.

(*And* ROONEY, *overwhelmed, starts screaming "Aggggghhhhh-hhhhh," a screaming-eagle sound, and making clawing eagle gestures at the air. He jumps up and down, stomping his feet.* COKES *instantly joins in, stomping and jumping and yelling.*)

ROONEY: Let's show these shit sacks how men are men jumpin' outa planes. Aggggggghhhhhhhhhh.

(*Stomping and yelling, they move in a circle,* ROONEY *followed by* COKES.)

A plane fulla yellin' stompin' men!

COKES: All yellin' stompin' men!

(*They yell and stomp, making eagle sounds, and then* ROONEY *leaps up on Billy's bed and runs the length of it until he is on the footlocker,* COKES *still on the floor, stomping.* ROONEY *makes a gesture of hooking his rip cord to the line inside the plane. They yell louder and louder and* ROONEY *leaps high into the air, yelling, "GERONIMO-O-O-O!" as* COKES *leaps onto the locker and then high into the air, bellowing, "GERONIMO-O-O-O!" They stand side by side, their arms held up in the air as if grasping the shroud lines of open chutes. They seem to float there in silence.*)

What a feelin' . . .

ROONEY: Beautiful feelin' . . .

(*For a moment more they float there, adrift in the room, the sky, their memory.* COKES *smiles at* ROONEY.)

COKES: Remember that one guy, O'Flannigan . . . ?
ROONEY (*nodding, smiling, remembering*): O'Flannigan . . .
COKES: He was this one guy . . . O'Flannigan . . .

(*He moves now toward the boys,* BILLY, ROGER *and* RICHIE, *who have gathered on Roger's bed and footlocker.* ROONEY *follows several steps, then drifts backward onto Billy's bed, where he sits and then lies back, listening to* COKES.)

We was testing chutes where you could just pull a lever by your ribs here when you hit the ground—see—and the chute would come off you, because it was just after a whole bunch a guys had been dragged to death in an unexpected and terrible wind at Fort Bragg. So they wanted you to be able to release the chute when you hit if there was a bad wind when you hit. So O'Flannigan was this kinda joker who had the goddamn sense a humor of a clown and nerves, I tell you, of steel, and he says he's gonna release the lever midair, then reach up, grab the lines and float on down, hanging. (*His hand paws at the air, seeking a rope that isn't there.*) So I seen him pull the lever at five hundred feet and he reaches up to two fistfuls a air, the chute's twenty feet above him, and he went into the ground like a knife.

(*The bottle, held high over his head, falls through the air to the bed, all watching it.*)

BILLY: Geezus.
ROONEY (*nodding gently*): Didn't get to sing the song, I bet.
COKES (*standing, staring at the fallen bottle*): No way.
RICHIE: What song?
ROONEY (*rises up, mysteriously angry*): Shit sack! Shit sack!
RICHIE: What song, Sergeant Rooney?
ROONEY: "Beautiful Streamer," shit sack.

(COKES, *gone into another reverie, is staring skyward.*)

COKES: I saw this one guy—never forget it. Never.
BILLY: That's Richie, Sergeant Rooney. He's a beautiful screamer.
RICHIE: He said "streamer," not "screamer," asshole.

(COKES *is still in his reverie.*)

COKES: This guy with his chute goin' straight up above him in a streamer, like a tulip, only white, you know. All twisted and never gonna open. Like a big icicle sticking straight up above him. He went right by me. We met eyes, sort of. He was lookin' real puzzled. He looks right at me. Then he looks up in the air at the chute, then down at the ground.

ROONEY: Did HE sing it?

COKES: He didn't sing it. He started going like this. (*He reaches desperately upward with both hands and begins to claw at the sky while his legs pump up and down.*) Like he was gonna climb right up the air.

RICHIE: Ohhhhh, Geezus.

BILLY: God.

(ROONEY *has collapsed backward on Billy's bed and he lies there and then he rises.*)

ROONEY: Cokes got the Silver Star for rollin' a barrel a oil down a hill in Korea into forty-seven chinky Chinese gooks who were climbin' up the hill and when he shot into it with his machine gun, it blew them all to grape jelly.

(COKES, *rocking a little on his feet, begins to hum and then sing "Beautiful Streamer," to the tune of Stephen Foster's "Beautiful Dreamer."*)

COKES: "Beautiful streamer, open for me . . . The sky is above me . . ." (*And then the singing stops.*) But the one I remember is this little guy in his spider hole, which is a hole in the ground with a lid over it. (*And he is using Richie's footlocker before him as the spider hole. He has fixed on it, is moving toward it.*) And he shot me in the ass as I was runnin' by, but the bullet hit me so hard— (*his body kind of jerks and he runs several steps*)—it knocked me into this ditch where he couldn't see me. I got behind him. (*Now at the head of Richie's bed, he begins to creep along the side of the bed as if sneaking up on the footlocker.*) Crawlin'. And I dropped a grenade into his hole. (*He jams a whiskey bottle into the footlocker, then slams down the lid.*)

Then sat on the lid, him bouncin' and yellin' under me. Bouncin' and yellin' under the lid. I could hear him. Feel him. I just sat there.

34 DAVID RABE

(Silence. ROONEY waits, thinking, then leans forward.)

ROONEY: He was probably singin' it.
COKES *(sitting there)*: I think so.
ROONEY: You think we should let 'em hear it?
BILLY: We're good boys. We're good ole boys.
COKES *(jerking himself to his feet, staggers sideways to join ROONEY on Billy's bed)*: I don't care who hears it, I just wanna be singin' it.

(ROONEY rises; he goes to the boys on Roger's bed and speaks to them carefully, as if lecturing people on something of great importance.)

ROONEY: You listen up; you just be listenin' up, 'cause if you hear it right you can maybe stop bein' shit sacks. This is what a man sings, he's goin' down through the air, his chute don't open.

(Flopping back down on the bunk beside COKES, ROONEY looks at COKES and then at the boys. The two older men put their arms around each other and they begin to sing.)

ROONEY AND COKES *(singing)*:

> Beautiful streamer,
> Open for me,
> The sky is above me,
> But no canopy.

BILLY *(murmuring)*: I don't believe it.
ROONEY AND COKES:

> Counted ten thousand,
> Pulled on the cord.
> My chute didn't open,
> I shouted, "Dear Lord."
>
> Beautiful streamer,
> This looks like the end,
> The earth is below me,
> My body won't end.
>
> Just like a mother
> Watching o'er me,
> Beautiful streamer,
> Ohhhhh, open for me.

ROGER: Un-fuckin'-believable.

ROONEY (*beaming with pride*): Ain't that a beauty.

(*And then* COKES *topples forward onto his face and flops limply to his side. The three boys leap to their feet.* ROONEY *lunges toward* COKES.)

RICHIE: Sergeant!

ROONEY: Cokie! Cokie!

BILLY: Jesus.

ROGER: Hey!

COKES: Huh? Huh? (*He sits up.* ROONEY *is kneeling beside him.*)

ROONEY: Jesus, Cokie.

COKES: I been doin' that; I been doin' that. It don't mean nothin'.

ROONEY: No, no.

COKES: (*pushing at* ROONEY, *who is trying to help him get back to the bed;* ROONEY *agrees with everything* COKES *is now saying, and the noises he makes are little animal noises*): I told 'em when they wanted to send me back I ain't got no leukemia; they wanna check it. They think I got it. I don't think I got it. Rooney? Whata you think?

ROONEY: No.

COKES: My mother had it. She had it. Just 'cause she did and I been fallin' down.

ROONEY: It don't mean nothin'.

COKES (*lunges back and up onto the bed*): I tole 'em I fall down 'cause I'm drunk. I'm drunk all the time.

ROONEY: You'll be goin' back over there with me, is what I know, Cokie. (*He is patting* COKES, *nodding, dusting him off.*) That's what I know.

(BILLY *comes up to them, almost seeming to want to be a part of the intimacy they are sharing.*)

BILLY: That was somethin', Sergeant Cokes. Jesus.

(ROONEY *whirls on him, ferocious, pushing him.*)

ROONEY: Get the fuck away, Wilson! Whata you know? Get the fuck away. You don't know shit. Get away! You don't know shit. (*And he turns to* COKES, *who is standing up from the bed.*) Me and Cokes are goin' to the war zone like we oughta. Gonna blow it to shit. (*He is grabbing at* COKES, *who is laughing. They are both laughing.* ROONEY *whirls on the boys.*) Ohhh, I'm gonna be so happy to be away from you assholes; you pussies. Not one regular army people among you possible. I swear it to my mother who is holy. You just be watchin' the papers for doin' darin' brave deeds. 'Cause we're old hands at it. Makin' shit disappear. Goddamn whooosh!

COKES: Whooosh!

ROONEY: Demnalitions. Me and . . . (*And then he knows he hasn't said it right.*) Me and Cokie . . . Demnal . . . Demnali . . .

RICHIE (*still sitting on* ROGER'S *bed*): You can do it, Sergeant.

BILLY: Get it. (*He stands by the lockers and* ROONEY *glares at him.*)

ROGER: 'Cause you're cool with dynamite, is what you're tryin' to say.

ROONEY (*charging at* ROGER, *bellowing*): Shut the fuck up, that's what you can do; and go to goddamn sleep. You buncha shit . . . sacks. Buncha mothers—know-it-all motherin' shit sacks— that's what you are.

COKES (*shoulders back, he is taking charge*): Just goin' to sleep is what you can do, 'cause Rooney and me fought it through two wars already and we can make it through this one more and leukemia that comes or doesn't come—who gives a shit? Not guys like us. We're goin' just pretty as pie. And it's lights-out time, ain't it, Rooney?

ROONEY: Past it, goddammit. So the lights are goin' out.

(*There is fear in the room, and the three boys rush to their wall lockers, where they start to strip to their underwear, preparing for bed.* ROONEY *paces the room, watching them, glaring.*)

Somebody's gotta teach you soldierin'. You hear me? Or you wanna go outside and march around awhile, huh? We can do that if you wanna. Huh? You tell me? Marchin' or sleepin'? What's it gonna be?

RICHIE (*rushing to get into bed*): Flick out the ole lights, Sergeant; that's what we say.

BILLY (*climbing into bed*): Put out the ole lights.

ROGER (*in bed and pulling up the covers*): Do it.

COKES: Shut up. (*He rocks forward and back, trying to stand at attention. He is saying good night.*) And that's an order. Just shut up. I got grenades down the hall. I got a pistol. I know where to get nitro. You don't shut up, I'll blow . . . you . . . to . . . fuck.

(*Making a military left-face, he stalks to the wall switch and turns the lights out. ROONEY is watching proudly, as COKES faces the boys again. He looks at them.*)

That's right.

(*In the dark, there is only a spill of light from the hall coming in the open door. COKES and ROONEY put their arms around each other and go out the door, leaving it partly open. RICHIE, ROGER and BILLY lie in their bunks, staring. They do not move. They lie there. The sergeants seem to have vanished soundlessly once they went out the door. Light touches each of the boys as they lie there.*)

ROGER (*does not move*): Lord have mercy, if that ain't a pair. If that ain't one pair a beauties.

BILLY: Oh, yeh. (*He does not move.*)

ROGER: Too much, man—too, too much.

RICHIE: They made me sad; but I loved them, sort of. Better than movies.

ROGER: Too much. Too, too much. (*Silence.*)

BILLY: What time is it?

ROGER: Sleep time, men. Sleep time. (*Silence.*)

BILLY: Right.

ROGER: They were somethin'. Too much.

BILLY: Too much.

RICHIE: Night.

ROGER: Night. (*Silence.*) Night, Billy.

BILLY: Night.

(*RICHIE stirs in his bed. ROGER turns onto his side. BILLY is motionless.*)

I . . . had a buddy, Rog—and this is the whole thing, this is the whole point—a kid I grew up with, played ball with in high school, and he was a tough little cat, a real bad man sometimes.

Used to have gangster pictures up in his room. Anyway, we got
into this deal where we'd drive on down to the big city, man, you
know, hit the bad spots, let some queer pick us up . . . sort of . . .
long enough to buy us some good stuff. It was kinda the thing to
do for a while, and we all did it, the whole gang of us. So we'd let
these cats pick us up, most of 'em old guys, and they were hurtin'
and happy as hell to have us, and we'd get a lot of free booze,
maybe a meal, and we'd turn 'em on. Then pretty soon they'd ask
us did we want to go over to their place. Sure, we'd say, and order
one more drink, and then when we hit the street, we'd tell 'em to
kiss off. We'd call 'em fag and queer and jazz like that and tell 'em
to kiss off. And Frankie, the kid I'm tellin' you about, he had a
mean streak in him and if they gave us a bad time at all, he'd put
'em down. That's the way he was. So that kinda jazz went on and
on for sort of a long time and it was a good deal if we were low on
cash or needed a laugh and it went on for a while. And then
Frankie—one day he come up to me—and he says he was goin'
home with the guy he was with. He said, what the hell, what did
it matter? And he's sayin'—Frankie's sayin'—why don't I tag
along? What the hell, he's sayin', what does it matter who does it
to you, some broad or some old guy, you close your eyes, a mouth's
a mouth, it don't matter—that's what he's sayin'. I tried to talk
him out of it, but he wasn't hearin' anything I was sayin'. So the
next day, see, he calls me up to tell me about it. Okay, okay, he
says, it was a cool scene, he says; they played poker, a buck
minimum, and he made a fortune. Frankie was eatin' it up, man.
It was a pretty way to live, he says. So he stayed at it, and he had
this nice little girl he was goin' with at the time. You know the
way a real bad cat can sometimes do that—have a good little girl
who's crazy about him and he is for her, too, and he's a different
cat when he's with her?
ROGER: Uh-huh.

(*The hall light slants across Billy's face.*)

BILLY: Well, that was him and Linda, and then one day he dropped
    her, he cut her loose. He was hooked, man. He was into it, with
    no way he knew out—you understand what I'm sayin'? He had
    got his ass hooked. He had never thought he would and then one

day he woke up and he was on it. He just hadn't been told, that's
the way I figure it; somebody didn't tell him somethin' he shoulda
been told and he come to me wailin' one day, man, all broke up
and wailin', my boy Frankie, my main man, and he was a fag. He
was a faggot, black Roger, and I'm not lyin'. I am not lyin' to you.

ROGER: Damn.

BILLY: So that's the whole thing, man; that's the whole thing.

(*Silence. They lie there.*)

ROGER: Holy . . . Christ. Richie . . . you hear him? You hear what
he said?

RICHIE: He's a storyteller.

ROGER: What you mean?

RICHIE: I mean, he's a storyteller, all right; he tells stories, all right.

ROGER: What are we into now? You wanna end up like that friend a
his, or you don't believe what he said? Which are you sayin'?

(*The door bursts open. The sounds of machine guns and cannon are
being made by someone, and* CARLYLE, *drunk and playing, comes
crawling in.* ROGER, RICHIE, *and* BILLY *all pop up, startled, to look
at him.*)

Hey, hey, what's happenin'?

BILLY: Who's happenin'?

ROGER: You attackin' or you retreatin', man?

CARLYLE (*looking up; big grin*): Hey, baby . . . ? (*Continues shooting,
crawling. The three boys look at each other.*)

ROGER: What's happenin', man? Whatcha doin'?

CARLYLE: I dunno, soul; I dunno. Practicin' my duties, my new
abilities. (*Half-sitting, he flops onto his side, starts to crawl.*) The
low crawl, man; like I was taught in basic, that's what I'm doin'.
You gotta know your shit, man, else you get your ass blown so far
away you don't ever see it again. Oh, sure, you guys don't care. I
know it. You got it made. You got it made. I don't got it made. You
got a little home here, got friends, people to talk to. I got nothin'.
You got jobs they probably ain't ever gonna ship you out, you got
so important jobs. I got no job. They don't even wanna give me a
job. I know it. They are gonna kill me. They are gonna send me

over there to get me killed, goddammit. WHATSAMATTER
WITH ALL YOU PEOPLE?

(*The anger explodes out of the grieving, and* ROGER *rushes to kneel
beside* CARLYLE. *He speaks gently, firmly.*)

ROGER: Hey, man, get cool, get some cool; purchase some cool, man.
CARLYLE: Awwwww . . . (*Clumsily, he turns away.*)
ROGER: Just hang in there.
CARLYLE: I don't wanna be no DEAD man. I don't wanna be the one
they all thinkin' is so stupid he's the only one'll go, they tell him;
they don't even have to give him a job. I got thoughts, man, in my
head; alla time, burnin', burnin' thoughts a understandin'.
ROGER: Don't you think we know that, man? It ain't the way you're
sayin' it.
CARLYLE: It is.
ROGER: No. I mean, we all probably gonna go. We all probably
gonna have to go.
CARLYLE: No-o-o-o-o.
ROGER: I mean it.
CARLYLE (*as he suddenly nearly topples over*): I am very drunk. (*And he
looks up at* ROGER.) You think so?
ROGER: I'm sayin' so. And I am sayin', "No sweat." No point.

(CARLYLE *angrily pushes at* ROGER, *knocking him backward.*)

CARLYLE: Awwwww, dammit, dammit, mother . . . shit . . . it . . .
ohhhhhhh. (*Sliding to the floor, the rage and anguish softening into
only breathing.*) I mean it. I mean it. (*Silence. He lies there.*)
ROGER: What . . . a you doin' . . . ?
CARLYLE: Huh?
ROGER: I don't know what you're up to on our freshly mopped floor.
CARLYLE: Gonna go sleep—okay? No sweat . . . (*Suddenly very
polite, he is looking up.*) Can I, soul? Izzit all right?
ROGER: Sure, man, sure, if you wanna, but why don't you go where
you got a bed? Don't you like beds?
CARLYLE: Dunno where's zat. My bed. I can' fin' it. I can' fin' my
own bed. I looked all over, but I can' fin' it anywhere. GONE!
(*Slipping back down now, he squirms to make a nest. He hugs his
bottle.*)

ROGER: (*moving to his bunk, where he grabs a blanket*): Okay, okay, man. But get on top a this, man. (*He is spreading the blanket on the floor, trying to help* CARLYLE *get on it.*) Make it softer. C'mon, c'mon . . . get on this.

(BILLY *has risen with his own blanket, and is moving now to hand it to* ROGER.)

BILLY: Cat's hurtin', Rog.

ROGER: Ohhhhh, yeh.

CARLYLE: Ohhhhh . . . it was so sweet at home . . . it was so sweet, baby; so-o-o good. They doin' dances make you wanna cry. . . . (*Hugging the blankets now, he drifts in a kind of dream.*)

ROGER: I know, man.

CARLYLE: So sweet . . . !

(BILLY *is moving back to his own bed, where, quietly, he sits.*)

ROGER: I know, man.

CARLYLE: So sweet . . . !

ROGER: Yeh.

CARLYLE: How come I gotta be here?

(*On his way to the door to close it,* ROGER *falters, looks at* CARLYLE, *then moves on toward the door.*)

ROGER: I dunno, Jim.

(BILLY *is sitting and watching, as* ROGER *goes on to the door, gently closes it, and returns to his bed.*)

BILLY: I know why he's gotta be here, Roger. You wanna know? Why don't you ask me?

ROGER: Okay. How come he gotta be here?

BILLY (*smiling*): Freedom's frontier, man. That's why.

ROGER (*settled on the edge of his bed and about to lie back*): Oh . . . yeh . . .

(*As a distant bugle begins to play taps and* RICHIE, *carrying a blanket, is approaching* CARLYLE. ROGER *settles back;* BILLY *is staring at* RICHIE; CARLYLE *does not stir; the bugle plays.*)

Bet that ole sarge don't live a year, Billy. Fuckin' blow his own ass sky high.

(RICHIE *has covered* CARLYLE. *He pats Carlyle's arm, and then straightens in order to return to his bed.*)

BILLY: Richie . . . !

(*Billy's hissing voice freezes* RICHIE. *He stands, and then he starts again to move, and* BILLY'S *voice comes again and* RICHIE *cannot move.*)

Richie . . . how come you gotta keep doin' that stuff?

(ROGER *looks at* BILLY, *staring at* RICHIE, *who stands still as a stone over the sleeping* CARLYLE.)

How come?

ROGER: He dunno, man. Do you? You dunno, do you, Rich?
RICHIE: No.
CARLYLE (*from deep in his sleep and grieving*): It . . . was . . . so . . . pretty . . . !
RICHIE: No.

(*The lights are fading with the last soft notes of taps.*)

ACT TWO

Scene One

Lights come up on the cadre room. It is late afternoon and BILLY *is lying on his stomach, his head at the foot of the bed, his chin resting on his hands. He wears gym shorts and sweat socks; his T-shirt lies on the bed and his sneakers are on the floor.* ROGER *is at his footlocker, taking out a pair of sweat socks. His sneakers and his basketball are on his bed. He is wearing his khakis.*

A silence passes, and then ROGER *closes his footlocker and sits on his bed, where he starts lacing his sneakers, holding them on his lap.*

BILLY: Rog . . . you think I'm a busybody? In any way? (*Silence.* ROGER *laces his sneakers.*) Roger?

ROGER: Huh? Uh-uh.

BILLY: Some people do. I mean, back home. (*He rolls slightly to look at* ROGER.) Or that I didn't know how to behave. Sort of.

ROGER: It's time we maybe get changed, don't you think? (*He rises and goes to his locker. He takes off his trousers, shoes and socks.*)

BILLY: Yeh. I guess. I don't feel like it, though. I don't feel good, don't know why.

ROGER: Be good for you, man; be good for you. (*Pulling on his gym shorts, he returns to his bed, carrying his shoes and socks.*)

BILLY: Yeh. (*He sits up on the edge of his bed.* ROGER, *sitting, is bowed over, putting on his socks.*) I mean, a lot a people thought like I didn't know how to behave in a simple way. You know? That I overcomplicated everything. I didn't think so. Don't think so. I just thought I was seein' complications that were there but nobody else saw. (*He is struggling now to put on his T-shirt. He seems weary, almost weak.*) I mean, Wisconsin's a funny place. All those clear-eyed people sayin' "Hello" and lookin' you straight in the eye. Everybody's good, you think, and happy and honest. And then there's all of a sudden a neighbor who goes mad as a hatter. I had a neighbor who came out of his house one morning with axes in both hands. He started then attackin' the cars that were driving up and down in front of his house. An' we all knew why he did it, sorta. (*He pauses; he thinks.*) It made me wanna be a priest. I wanted to be a priest then. I was sixteen. Priests could help people. Could take away what hurt 'em. I wanted that, I thought. Somethin', huh?

ROGER (*has the basketball in his hands*): Yeh. But everybody's got feelin's like that sometimes.

BILLY: I don't know.

ROGER: You know, you oughta work on a little jump shot, my man. Get you some kinda fall-away jumper to go with that beauty of a hook. Make you tough out there.

BILLY: Can't fuckin' do it. Not my game. I mean, like that bar we go to. You think I could get a job there bartendin', maybe? I could learn the ropes. (*He is watching* ROGER, *who has risen to walk to his locker.*) You think I could get a job there off-duty hours?

ROGER (*pulling his locker open to display the pinup on the inside of the door*): You don't want no job. It's that little black-haired waitress you wantin' to know.

BILLY: No, man. Not really.

ROGER: It's okay. She tough, man. (*He begins to remove his uniform shirt. He will put on an O.D. T-shirt to go to the gym.*)

BILLY: I mean, not the way you're sayin' it, is all. Sure, there's somethin' about her. I don't know what. I ain't even spoke to her yet. But somethin'. I mean, what's she doin' there? When she's dancin', it's like she knows somethin'. She's degradin' herself, I sometimes feel. You think she is?

ROGER: Man, you don't even know the girl. She's workin'.

BILLY: I'd like to talk to her. Tell her stuff. Find out about her. Sometimes I'm thinkin' about her and I got a job there, I get to know her and she and I get to be real tight, man—close, you know. Maybe we screw, maybe we don't. It's nice . . . whatever.

ROGER: Sure. She a real fine-lookin' chippy, Billy. Got nice cakes. Nice little titties.

BILLY: I think she's smart, too.

(ROGER *starts laughing so hard he almost falls into his locker.*)

Oh, all I do is talk. "Yabba-yabba." I mean, my mom and dad are really terrific people. How'd they ever end up with somebody so weird as me?

(ROGER *moves to him, jostles him.*)

ROGER: I'm tellin' you, the gym and a little ball is what you need. Little exercise. Little bumpin' into people. The soul is tellin' you.

(BILLY *rises and goes to his locker, where he starts putting on his sweat clothes.*)

BILLY: I mean, Roger, you remember how we met in P Company? Both of us brand-new. You started talkin' to me. You just started talkin' to me and you didn't stop.

ROGER (*hardly looking up*): Yeh.

BILLY: Did you see somethin' in me made you pick me?

ROGER: I was talkin' to everybody, man. For that whole day. Two whole days. You was just the first one to talk back friendly. Though you didn't say much, as I recall.

BILLY: The first white person, you mean. (*Wearing his sweatpants, he is now at his bed, putting on his sneakers.*)

ROGER: Yeh. I was tryin' to come outa myself a little. Do like the fuckin' headshrinker been tellin' me to stop them fuckin' headaches I was havin', you know. Now let us do fifteen or twenty push-ups and get over to that gymnasium, like I been sayin'. Then we can take our civvies with us—we can shower and change at the gym. (*He crosses to* BILLY, *who flops down on his belly on the bed.*)

BILLY: I don't know . . . I don't know what it is I'm feelin'. Sick like.

(ROGER *forces* BILLY *up onto his feet and shoves him playfully downstage, where they both fall forward into the push-up position, side by side.*)

ROGER: Do 'em, trooper. Do 'em. Get it.

(ROGER *starts.* BILLY *joins in. After five,* ROGER *realizes that* BILLY *has his knees on the floor. They start again. This time,* BILLY *counts in double time. They start again. At about "seven,"* RICHIE *enters. Neither* BILLY *nor* ROGER *sees him. They keep going.*)

ROGER AND BILLY: . . . seven, eight, nine, ten . . .
RICHIE: No, no; no, no; no, no, no. That's not it; that's not it.

(*They keep going, yelling the numbers louder and louder.*)

ROGER AND BILLY: . . . eleven, twelve, thirteen . . .

(RICHIE *crosses to his locker and gets his bottle of cologne, and then returning to the center of the room to stare at them, he stands there dabbing cologne on his face.*)

ROGER AND BILLY: . . . fourteen, fifteen.
RICHIE: You'll never get it like that. You're so far apart and you're both humping at the same time. And all that counting. It's so unromantic.
ROGER (*rising and moving to his bed to pick up the basketball*): We was exercisin', Richard. You heard a that?
RICHIE: Call it what you will, Roger.

(*With a flick of his wrist,* ROGER *tosses the basketball to* BILLY.)

Everybody has their own cute little pet names for it.

BILLY: Hey!

(*And he tosses the ball at* RICHIE, *hitting him in the chest, sending the cologne bottle flying.* RICHIE *yelps, as* BILLY *retrieves the ball and, grabbing up his sweat jacket from the bed, heads for the door.* ROGER, *at his own locker, has taken out his suit bag of civilian clothes.*)

You missed.

RICHIE: Billy, Billy, Billy, please, please, the ruffian approach will not work with me. It impresses me not even one tiny little bit. All you've done is spill my cologne. (*He bends to pick up the cologne from the floor.*)
BILLY: That was my aim.
ROGER: See you.

(BILLY *is passing* RICHIE. *Suddenly* RICHIE *sprays* BILLY *with cologne, some of it getting on* ROGER, *as* ROGER *and* BILLY, *groaning and cursing at* RICHIE, *rush out the door.*)

RICHIE: Try the more delicate approach next time, Bill.

(*Having crossed to the door, he stands a moment, leaning against the frame. Then he bounces to Billy's bed, sings "He's just my Bill," and squirts cologne on the pillow. At his locker, he deposits the cologne, takes off his shirt, shoes, and socks. Removing a hardcover copy of* Pauline Kael's I Lost It at the Movies *from the top shelf of the locker, he bounds to the center of the room and tosses the book the rest of the way to the bed. Quite pleased with himself, he fidgets, pats his stomach, then lowers himself into the push-up position, goes to his knees, and stands up.*)

Am I out of my fucking mind? Those two are crazy. I'm not crazy.

(*He pivots and strides to his locker. With an ashtray, a pack of matches, and a pack of cigarettes, he hurries to his bed and makes himself comfortable to read, his head propped up on a pillow. Settling himself, he opens the book, finds his place, thinks a little, starts to read. For a moment he lies there. And then* CARLYLE *steps into the room. He comes through the doorway looking to his left and right. He comes several steps into the room and looks at* RICHIE. RICHIE *sees him. They look at each other.*)

CARLYLE: Ain't nobody here, man?
RICHIE: Hello, Carlyle. How are you today?
CARLYLE: Ain't nobody here? (*He is nervous and angrily disappointed.*)
RICHIE: Who do you want?
CARLYLE: Where's the black boy?
RICHIE: Roger? My God, why do you keep calling him that? Don't you know his name yet? Roger. Roger. (*He thickens his voice at this, imitating someone very stupid.* CARLYLE *stares at him.*)
CARLYLE: Yeh. Where is he?
RICHIE: I am not his keeper, you know. I am not his private secretary, you know.
CARLYLE: I do not know. I do not know. That is why I am asking. I come to see him. You are here. I ask you. I don't know. I mean,

Carlyle made a fool outa himself comin' in here the other night, talkin' on and on like how he did. Lay on the floor. He remember. You remember? It all one hype, man; that all one hype. You know what I mean. That ain't the real Carlyle was in here. This one here and now the real Carlyle. Who the real Richie?

RICHIE: Well . . . the real Richie . . . has gone home. To Manhattan. I, however, am about to read this book. (*Which he again starts to try to do.*)

CARLYLE: Oh. Shit. Jus' you the only one here, then, huh?

RICHIE: So it would seem. (*He looks at the air and then under the bed as if to find someone.*) So it would seem. Did you hear about Martin?

CARLYLE: What happened to Martin? I ain't seen him.

RICHIE: They are shipping him home. Someone told about what he did to himself. I don't know who.

CARLYLE: Wasn't me. Not me. I keep that secret.

RICHIE: I'm sure you did. (*Rising, walking toward* CARLYLE *and the door, cigarette pack in hand.*) You want a cigarette? Or don't you smoke? Or do you have to go right away? (*Closing the door.*) There's a chill sometimes coming down the hall, I don't know from where. (*Crossing back to his bed and climbing in.*) And I think I've got the start of a little cold. Did you want the cigarette?

(CARLYLE *is staring at him. Then he examines the door and looks again at* RICHIE. *He stares at* RICHIE, *thinking, and then he walks toward him.*)

CARLYLE: You know what I bet? I been lookin' at you real close. It just a way I got about me. And I bet if I was to hang my boy out in front of you, my big boy, man, you'd start wantin' to touch him. Be beggin' and talkin' sweet to ole Carlyle. Am I right or wrong? (*He leans over* RICHIE.) What do you say?

RICHIE: Pardon?

CARLYLE: You heard me. Ohhh. I am so restless, I don't even understand it. My big black boy is what I was talkin' about. My thing, man; my rope, Jim. HEY, RICHIE! (*And he lunges, then moves his fingers through Richie's hair.*) How long you been a punk? Can you hear me? Am I clear? Do I talk funny? (*He is leaning close.*) Can you smell the gin on my mouth?

RICHIE: I mean, if you really came looking for Roger, he and Billy are gone to the gymnasium. They were—

CARLYLE: No. (*He slides down on the bed, his arm placed over Richie's legs.*) I got no athletic abilities. I got none. No moves. I don't know. HEY, RICHIE! (*Leaning close again.*) I just got this question I asked. I got no answer.

RICHIE: I don't know . . . what . . . you mean.

CARLYLE: I heard me. I understood me. "How long you been a punk?" is the question I asked. Have you got a reply?

RICHIE (*confused, irritated, but fascinated*): Not to that question.

CARLYLE: Who do if you don't? I don't. How'm I gonna?

(*Suddenly there is whistling in the hall, as if someone might enter, footsteps approaching, and* RICHIE *leaps to his feet and scurries away toward the door, tucking in his undershirt as he goes.*)

Man, don't you wanna talk to me? Don't you wanna talk to ole Carlyle?

RICHIE: Not at the moment.

CARLYLE (*rising, starting after* RICHIE, *who stands nervously near Roger's bed*): I want to talk to you, man; why don't you want to talk to me? We can be friends. Talkin' back and forth, sharin' thoughts and bein' happy.

RICHIE: I don't think that's what you want.

CARLYLE (*very near to* RICHIE): What do I want?

RICHIE: I mean, to talk to me. (*As if repulsed, he crosses away. But it is hard to tell if the move is genuine or coy.*)

CARLYLE: What am I doin'? I am talkin'. DON'T YOU TELL ME I AIN'T TALKIN' WHEN I AM TALKIN'! COURSE I AM. Bendin' over backwards. (*And pressing his hands against himself in his anger, he has touched the grease on his shirt, the filth of his clothing, and this ignites the anger.*) Do you know they still got me in that goddamn P Company? That goddamn transient company. It like they think I ain't got no notion what a home is. No nose for no home—like I ain't never had no home. I had a home. IT LIKE THEY THINK THERE AIN'T NO PLACE FOR ME IN THIS MOTHER ARMY BUT K.P. ALL SUDSY AND WRIN-KLED AND SWEATIN'. EVERY DAY SINCE I GOT TO

THIS SHIT HOUSE, MISTER! HOW MANY TIMES YOU BEEN ON K.P.? WHEN'S THE LAST TIME YOU PULLED K.P.? (*He has roared down to where* RICHIE *had moved, the rage possessing him.*)

RICHIE: I'm E.D.

CARLYLE: You E.D.? You E.D.? You Edie, are you? I didn't ask you what you friends call you, I asked you when's the last time you had K.P.?

RICHIE (*edging toward his bed; he will go there, get and light a cigarette*): E.D. is "Exempt from Duty."

CARLYLE (*moving after* RICHIE): You ain't got no duties? What shit you talkin' about? Everybody in this fuckin' army got duties. That what the fuckin' army all about. You ain't got no duties, who got 'em?

RICHIE: Because of my job, Carlyle. I have a very special job. And my friends don't call me Edie. (*Big smile.*) They call me Irene.

CARLYLE: That mean what you sayin' is you kiss ass for somebody, don't it? Good for you. (*Seemingly relaxed and gentle, he settles down on Richie's bed. He seems playful and charming.*) You know the other night I was sleepin' there. You know.

RICHIE: Yes.

CARLYLE (*gleefully, enormously pleased*): You remember that? How come you remember that? You sweet.

RICHIE: We don't have people sleeping on our floor that often, Carlyle.

CARLYLE: But the way you crawl over in the night, gimme a big kiss on my joint. That nice.

RICHIE (*shocked, he blinks*): What?

CARLYLE: Or did I dream that?

RICHIE (*laughing in spite of himself*): My God, you're outrageous!

CARLYLE: Maybe you dreamed it.

RICHIE: What . . . ? No. I don't know.

CARLYLE: Maybe you did it, then; you didn't dream it.

RICHIE: How come you talk so much?

CARLYLE: I don't talk, man, who's gonna talk? YOU? (*He is laughing and amused, but there is an anger near the surface now, an ugliness.*) That bore me to death. I don't like nobody's voice but my own. I am so pretty. Don't like nobody else face. (*And then viciously, he*

spits out at RICHIE.) You goddamn face ugly fuckin' queer punk!
(*And* RICHIE *jumps in confusion.*)

RICHIE: What's the matter with you?

CARLYLE: You goddamn ugly punk face. YOU UGLY!

RICHIE: Nice mouth.

CARLYLE: That's right. That's right. And you got a weird mouth. Like to suck joints.

(*As* RICHIE *storms to his locker, throwing the book inside. He pivots, grabbing a towel, marching toward the door.*)

Hey, you gonna jus' walk out on me? Where you goin'? You c'mon back. Hear?

RICHIE: That's my bed, for chrissake. (*He lunges into the hall.*)

CARLYLE: You'd best. (*Lying there, he makes himself comfortable. He takes a pint bottle from his back pocket.*) You come back, Richie, I tell you a good joke. Make you laugh, make you cry. (*He takes a big drink.*) That's right. Ole Frank and Jesse, they got the stagecoach stopped, all the peoples lined up—Frank say, "All right, peoples, we gonna rape all the men and rob all the women." Jesse say, "Frank, no, no—that ain't it—we gonna—" And this one little man yell real loud, "You shut up, Jesse; Frank knows what he's doin'."

(*Loudly, he laughs and laughs.* BILLY *enters. Startled at the sight of* CARLYLE *there in Richie's bed,* BILLY *falters, as* CARLYLE *gestures toward him.*)

Hey, man . . . ! Hey, you know, they send me over to that Vietnam, I be cool, 'cause I been dodgin' bullets and shit since I been old enough to get on pussy make it happy to know me. I can get on, I can do my job.

(BILLY *looks weary and depressed. Languidly he crosses to his bed. He still wears his sweat clothes.* CARLYLE *studies him, then stares at the ceiling.*)

Yeh. I was just layin' here thinkin' that and you come in and out it come, words to say my feelin'. That my problem. That the black man's problem altogether. You ever considered that? Too

much feelin'. He too close to everything. He is, man; too close to
his blood, to his body. It ain't that he don't have no good mind,
but he BELIEVE in his body. Is . . . that Richie the only punk in
this room, or is there more?

BILLY: What?

CARLYLE: The punk; is he the only punk? (*Carefully he takes one of
Richie's cigarettes and lights it.*)

BILLY: He's all right.

CARLYLE: I ain't askin' about the quality of his talent, but is he the
only one, is my question?

BILLY (*does not want to deal with this; he sits there*): You get your orders
yet?

CARLYLE: Orders for what?

BILLY: To tell you where you work.

CARLYLE: I'm P Company, man. I work in P Company. I do K.P.
That all. Don't deserve no more. Do you know I been in this
army three months and ten days and everybody still doin' the same
shit and sayin' the same shit and wearin' the same green shitty
clothes? I ain't been happy one day, and that a lotta goddamn
misery back to back in this ole boy. Is that Richie a good punk?
Huh? Is he? He takes care of you and Roger—that how come you
in this room, the three of you?

BILLY: What?

CARLYLE (*emphatically*): You and Roger are hittin' on Richie, right?

BILLY: He's not queer, if that's what you're sayin'. A little effemi-
nate, but that's all, no more; if that's what you're sayin'.

CARLYLE: I'd like to get some of him myself if he a good punk, is
what I'm sayin'. That's what I'm sayin'! You don't got no understandin' how a man can maybe be a little diplomatic about what
he's sayin' sorta sideways, do you? Jesus.

BILLY: He don't do that stuff.

CARLYLE (*lying there*): What stuff?

BILLY: Listen, man. I don't feel too good, you don't mind.

CARLYLE: What stuff?

BILLY: What you're thinkin'.

CARLYLE: What . . . am I thinkin'?

BILLY: You . . . know.

CARLYLE: Yes, I do. It in my head, that how come I know. But how do you know? I can see your heart, Billy boy, but you cannot see mine. I am unknown. You . . . are known.

BILLY (*as if he is about to vomit, and fighting it*): You just . . . talk fast and keep movin', don't you? Don't ever stay still.

CARLYLE: Words to say my feelin', Billy boy.

(RICHIE *steps into the room. He sees* BILLY *and* CARLYLE, *and freezes.*)

There he is. There he be.

(RICHIE *moves to his locker to put away the towel.*)

RICHIE: He's one of them who hasn't come down far out of the trees yet, Billy; believe me.

CARLYLE: You got rudeness in your voice, Richie—you got meanness I can hear about ole Carlyle. You tellin' me I oughta leave— is that what you think you're doin'? You don't want me here?

RICHIE: You come to see Roger, who isn't here, right? Man like you must have important matters to take care of all over the quad; I can't imagine a man like you not having extremely important things to do all over the world, as a matter of fact, Carlyle.

CARLYLE (*rises, begins to smooth the sheets and straighten the pillow; he will put the pint bottle in his back pocket and cross near to* RICHIE): Ohhhh, listen—don't mind all the shit I say. I just talk bad, is all I do; I don't do bad. I got to have friends just like anybody else. I'm just bored and restless, that all; takin' it out on you two. I mean, I know Richie here ain't really no punk, not really. I was just talkin', just jivin' and entertainin' my own self. Don't take me serious, not ever. I get on out and see you all later. (*He moves for the door,* RICHIE *right behind him, almost ushering him.*) You be cool, hear? Man don't do the jivin', he the one gettin' jived. That what my little brother Henry tell me and tell me.

(*Moving leisurely,* CARLYLE *backs out the door and is gone.* RICHIE *shuts the door. There is a silence as* RICHIE *stands by the door.* BILLY *looks at him and then looks away.*)

BILLY: I am gonna have to move myself outa here, Roger decides to adopt that sonofabitch.

RICHIE: He's an animal.

BILLY: Yeh, and on top a that, he's a rotten person.

RICHIE (*laughs nervously, crossing nearer to* BILLY): I think you're probably right.

(*Still laughing a little,* RICHIE *pats Billy's shoulder and* BILLY *freezes at the touch. Awkwardly,* RICHIE *removes his hand and crosses to his bed. When he has lain down,* BILLY *bends to take off his sneakers, then lies back on his pillow staring, thinking, and there is a silence.* RICHIE *does not move. He lies there, struggling to prepare himself for something.*)

Hey . . . Billy? (*Very slight pause.*) Billy?

BILLY: Yeh.

RICHIE: You know that story you told the other night?

BILLY: Yeh . . . ?

RICHIE: You know . . .

BILLY: What . . . about it?

RICHIE: Well, was it . . . about you? (*Pause.*) I mean, was it . . . ABOUT you? Were you Frankie? (*This is difficult for him.*) Are . . . you Frankie? Billy? (BILLY *is slowly sitting up.*)

BILLY: You sonofabitch . . . !

RICHIE: Or was it really about somebody you knew . . . ?

BILLY (*sitting, outraged and glaring*): You didn't hear me at all!

RICHIE: I'm just asking a simple question, Billy, that's all I'm doing.

BILLY: You are really sick. You know that? Your brain is really, truly rancid! Do you know there's a theory now it's genetic? That it's all a matter of genes and shit like that?

RICHIE: Everything is not so ungodly cryptic, Billy.

BILLY: You. You, man, and the rot it's makin' outa your feeble fuckin' brain.

(ROGER, *dressed in civilian clothes, bursts in and* BILLY *leaps to his feet.*)

ROGER: Hey, hey, anyone got a couple bucks he can loan me?

BILLY: Rog, where you been?

ROGER (*throwing the basketball and his sweat clothes into his locker*): I need five. C'mon.

BILLY: Where you been? That asshole friend a yours was here.

ROGER: I know, I know. Can you gimme five?

RICHIE (*jumps to the floor and heads for his locker*): You want five. I got it. You want ten or more, even?

(BILLY, *watching* RICHIE, *turns, and nervously paces down right, where he moves about, worried.*)

BILLY: I mean, we gotta talk about him, man; we gotta talk about him.

ROGER (*as* RICHIE *is handing him two fives*): 'Cause we goin' to town together. I jus' run into him out on the quad, man, and he was feelin' real bad 'bout the way he acted, how you guys done him, he was fallin' down apologizin' all over the place.

BILLY (*as* RICHIE *marches back to his bed and sits down*): I mean, he's got a lotta weird ideas about us; I'm tellin' you.

ROGER: He's just a little fucked up in his head is all, but he ain't trouble. (*He takes a pair of sunglasses from the locker and puts them on.*)

BILLY: Who needs him? I mean, we don't need him.

ROGER: You gettin' too nervous, man. Nobody said anything about anybody needin' anybody. I been on the street all my life; he brings back home. I played me a little ball, Billy; took me a shower. I'm feelin' good! (*He has moved down to* BILLY.)

BILLY: I'm tellin' you there's something wrong with him, though.

ROGER (*face to face with* BILLY, *he is a little irritated*): Every black man in the world ain't like me, man; you get used to that idea. You get to know him, and you gonna like him. I'm tellin' you. You get to be laughin' just like me to hear him talk his shit. But you gotta relax.

RICHIE: I agree with Billy, Roger.

ROGER: Well, you guys got it all worked out and that's good, but I am goin' to town with him. Man's got wheels. Got a good head. You got any sense, you'll come with us.

BILLY: What are you talkin' about—come with you? I just tole you he's crazy.

ROGER: And I tole you you're wrong.

RICHIE: We weren't invited.

ROGER: I'm invitin' you.

RICHIE: No, I don't wanna.

ROGER (*moves to* RICHIE; *it seems he really wants* RICHIE *to go*): You sure, Richie? C'mon.

RICHIE: No.

ROGER: Billy? He got wheels, we goin' in drinkin', see if gettin' our heads real bad don't just make us feel real good. You know what I mean. I got him right; you got him wrong.

BILLY: But what if I'm right?

ROGER: Billy, Billy, the man is waitin' on me. You know you wanna. Jesus. Bad cat like that gotta know the way. He been to D.C. before. Got cousins here. Got wheels for the weekend. You always talkin' how you don't do nothin'—you just talk it. Let's do it tonight—stop talkin'. Be cruisin' up and down the strip, leanin' out the window, bad as we wanna be. True cool is a car. We can flip a cigarette out the window—we can watch it bounce. Get us some chippies. You know we can. And if we don't, he knows a cathouse, it fulla cats.

BILLY: You serious?

RICHIE: You mean you're going to a whorehouse? That's disgusting.

BILLY: Listen who's talkin'. What do you want me to do? Stay here with you?

RICHIE: We could go to a movie or something.

ROGER: I am done with this talkin'. You goin', you stayin'? (*He crosses to his locker, pulls into view a wide-brimmed black and shiny hat, and puts it on, cocking it at a sharp angle.*)

BILLY: I don't know.

ROGER (*stepping for the door*): I am goin'.

BILLY (*turning, he sees the hat*): I'm going. Okay! I'm going! Going, going, going! (*And he runs to his locker.*)

RICHIE: Oh, Billy, you'll be scared to death in a cathouse and you know it.

BILLY: BULLSHIT! (*He is removing his sweatpants and putting on a pair of gray corduroy trousers.*)

ROGER: Billy got him a lion tamer 'tween his legs!

(*The door bangs open and* CARLYLE *is there, still clad in his filthy fatigues, but wearing a going-to-town black knit cap on his head and carrying a bottle.*)

CARLYLE: Man, what's goin' on? I been waitin' like throughout my fuckin' life.

ROGER: Billy's goin', too. He's gotta change.

CARLYLE: He goin', too! Hey! Beautiful! That beautiful! (*His grin is large, his laugh is loud.*)

ROGER: Didn't I tell you, Billy?

CARLYLE: That beautiful, man; we all goin' to be friends!

RICHIE (*sitting on his bed*): What about me, Carlyle?

(CARLYLE *looks at* RICHIE, *and then at* ROGER, *and then he and* ROGER *begin to laugh.* CARLYLE *pokes* ROGER *and they laugh as they are leaving.* BILLY, *grabbing up his sneakers to follow, stops at the door, looking only briefly at* RICHIE. *Then* BILLY *goes and shuts the door. The lights are fading to black.*)

Scene Two

In the dark, taps begins to play. And then slowly the lights rise, but the room remains dim. Only the lamp attached to Richie's bed burns and there is the glow and spill of the hallway coming through the transom. BILLY, CARLYLE, ROGER, *and* RICHIE *are sprawled about the room.* BILLY, *lying on his stomach, has his head at the foot of his bed, a half-empty bottle of beer dangling in his hand. He wears a blue oxford-cloth shirt and his sneakers lie beside his bed.* ROGER, *collapsed in his own bed, lies upon his back, his head also at the foot, a* Playboy *magazine covering his face and a half-empty bottle of beer in his hands, folded on his belly. Having removed his civilian shirt, he wears a white T-shirt.* CARLYLE *is lying on his belly on Richie's bed, his head at the foot, and he is facing out.* RICHIE *is sitting on the floor, resting against Roger's footlocker. He is wrapped in a blanket. Beside him is an unopened bottle of beer and a bottle opener.*

They are all dreamy in the dimness as taps plays sadly on and then fades into silence. No one moves.

RICHIE: I don't know where it was, but it wasn't here. And we were all in it—it felt like—but we all had different faces. After you guys left, I only dozed for a few minutes, so it couldn't have been long. Roger laughed a lot and Billy was taller. I don't remember all the details exactly, and even though we were the ones in it, I know it was about my father. He was a big man. I was six. He was a very big man when I was six and he went away, but I remember him. He started drinking and staying home making model airplanes and boats and paintings by the numbers. We had money from mom's family, so he was just home all the time. And then one day I was coming home from kindergarten, and as I was starting up the front walk he came out the door and he had these suitcases in his hands. He was leaving, see, sneaking out, and I'd caught him. We looked at each other and I just knew and I started crying. He yelled at me, "Don't you cry; don't you start crying." I tried to grab him and he pushed me down in the grass. And then he was gone. G–O–N–E.

BILLY: And that was it? That was it?

RICHIE: I remember hiding my eyes. I lay in the grass and hid my eyes and waited.

BILLY: He never came back?

RICHIE: No.

CARLYLE: Ain't that some shit. Now, I'm a jive-time street nigger. I knew where my daddy was all the while. He workin' in this butcher shop two blocks up the street. Ole Mom used to point him out. "There he go. That him—that your daddy." We'd see him on the street, "There he go."

ROGER: Man couldn't see his way to livin' with you—that what you're sayin'?

CARLYLE: Never saw the day.

ROGER: And still couldn't get his ass outa the neighborhood?

(RICHIE *begins trying to open his bottle of beer.*)

CARLYLE: Ain't that a bitch. Poor ole bastard just duck his head— Mom pointin' at him—he git this real goddamn hangdog look like he don't know who we talkin' about and he walk a little faster. Why the hell he never move away I don't know, unless he was crazy. But I don't think so. He come up to me once—I was playin'. "Boy," he says, "I ain't your daddy. I ain't. Your momma's crazy." "Don't you be callin' my momma crazy, Daddy," I tole him. Poor ole thing didn't know what to do.

RICHIE (*giving up; he can't get the beer open*): Somebody open this for me? I can't get this open.

(BILLY *seems about to move to help, but* CARLYLE *is quicker, rising a little on the bunk and reaching.*)

CARLYLE: Ole Carlyle get it.

(RICHIE *slides along the floor until he can place the bottle in Carlyle's outstretched hand.*)

RICHIE: Then there was this once—there was this TV documentary about these bums in San Francisco, this TV guy interviewing all these bums, and just for maybe ten seconds while he was talkin' . . .

(*Smiling,* CARLYLE *hands* RICHIE *the opened bottle.*)

. . . to this one bum, there was this other one in the background jumpin' around like he thought he was dancin' and wavin' his hat, and even though there wasn't anything about him like my father and I didn't really ever see his face at all, I just kept thinkin': That's him. My dad. He thinks he's dancin'.

(*They lie there in silence and suddenly, softly,* BILLY *giggles, and then he giggles a little more and louder.*)

BILLY: Jesus!
RICHIE: What?
BILLY: That's ridiculous, Richie; sayin' that, thinkin' that. If it didn't look like him, it wasn't him, but you gotta be makin' up a story.
CARLYLE (*shifting now for a more comfortable position, he moves his head to the pillow at the top of the bed*): Richie first saw me, he didn't like me much nohow, but he thought it over now, he changed his way a thinkin'. I can see that clear. We gonna be one big happy family.

RICHIE: Carlyle likes me, Billy; he thinks I'm pretty.

CARLYLE (*sitting up a little to make his point clear*): No, I don't think you pretty. A broad is pretty. Punks ain't pretty. Punk—if he good-lookin'—is cute. You cute.

RICHIE: He's gonna steal me right away, little Billy. You're so slow, Bill. I prefer a man who's decisive. (*He is lying down now on the floor at the foot of his bed.*)

BILLY: You just keep at it, you're gonna have us all believin' you are just what you say you are.

RICHIE: Which is more than we can say for you.

(*Now* ROGER *rises on his elbow to light a cigarette.*)

BILLY: Jive, jive.

RICHIE: You're arrogant, Billy. So arrogant.

BILLY: What are you—on the rag?

RICHIE: Wouldn't it just bang your little balls if I were!

ROGER (*to* RICHIE): Hey, man. What's with you?

RICHIE: Stupidity offends me; lies and ignorance offend me.

BILLY: You know where we was? The three of us? All three of us, earlier on? To the wrong side of the tracks, Richard. One good black upside-down whorehouse where you get what you buy, no jive along with it—so if it's a lay you want and need, you go! Or don't they have faggot whorehouses?

ROGER: IF YOU GUYS DON'T CUT THIS SHIT OUT I'M GONNA BUST SOMEBODY'S HEAD! (*Angrily, he flops back on his bed. There is a silence as they all lie there.*)

RICHIE: "Where we was," he says. Listen to him. "Where we was." And he's got more school, Carlyle, than you have fingers and . . . (*He has lifted his foot onto the bed; it touches, presses, Carlyle's foot.*) . . . toes. It's this pseudo-earthy quality he feigns—but inside he's all cashmere.

BILLY: That's a lie. (*Giggling, he is staring at the floor.*) I'm polyester, worsted and mohair.

RICHIE: You have a lot of school, Billy; don't say you don't.

BILLY: You said "fingers and toes"; you didn't say "a lot."

CARLYLE: I think people get dumber the more they put their butts into some schoolhouse door.

BILLY: It depends on what the hell you're talkin' about. (*Now he looks at* CARLYLE, *and sees the feet touching.*)

CARLYLE: I seen cats back on the block, they knew what was shakin'—then they got into all this school jive and, man, every year they went, they come back they didn't know nothin'.

(BILLY *is staring at Richie's foot pressed against and rubbing Carlyle's foot.* RICHIE *sees* BILLY *looking.* BILLY *cannot believe what he is seeing. It fills him with fear. The silence goes on and on.*)

RICHIE: Billy, why don't you and Roger go for a walk?

BILLY: What? (*He bolts to his knees. He is frozen on his knees on the bed.*)

RICHIE: Roger asked you to go downtown, you went, you had fun.

ROGER (*having turned, he knows almost instantly what is going on*): I asked you, too.

RICHIE: You asked me; you BEGGED Billy. I said no. Billy said no. You took my ten dollars. You begged Billy. I'm asking you a favor now—go for a walk. Let Carlyle and me have some time. (*Silence.*)

CARLYLE (*sits up, uneasy and wary*): That how you work it?

ROGER: Work what?

CARLYLE: Whosever turn it be.

BILLY: No, no, that ain't the way we work it, because we don't work it.

CARLYLE: See? See? There it is—that goddamn education showin' through. All them years in school. Man, didn't we have a good time tonight? You rode in my car. I showed you a good cathouse, all that sweet black pussy. Ain't we friends? Richie likes me. How come you don't like me?

BILLY: 'Cause if you really are doin' what I think you're doin', you're a fuckin' animal!

(CARLYLE *leaps to his feet, hand snaking to his pocket to draw a weapon.*)

ROGER: Billy, no.

BILLY: NO, WHAT?!

ROGER: Relax, man; no need. (*He turns to* CARLYLE; *patiently, wearily, he speaks.*) Man, I tole you it ain't goin' on here. We both tole you it ain't goin' on here.

CARLYLE: Don't you jive me, nigger. You goin' for a walk like I'm askin', or not? I wanna get this clear.

ROGER: Man, we live here.

RICHIE: It's my house, too, Roger; I live here, too. (*He bounds to his feet, flinging the blanket that has been covering him so it flies and lands on the floor near Roger's footlocker.*)

ROGER: Don't I know that? Did I say somethin' to make you think I didn't know that?

(*Standing, RICHIE is removing his trousers and throwing them down on his footlocker.*)

RICHIE: Carlyle is my guest.

(*Sitting down on the side of his bed and facing out, he puts his arms around Carlyle's thigh. ROGER jumps to his feet and grabs the blanket from the foot of his bed. Shaking it open, he drops onto the bed, his head at the foot of the bed and facing off as he covers himself.*)

ROGER: Fine. He your friend. This your home. So that mean he can stay. It don't mean I gotta leave. I'll catch you all in the mornin'.

BILLY: Roger, what the hell are you doin'?

ROGER: What you better do, Billy. It's gettin' late. I'm goin' to sleep.

BILLY: What?

ROGER: Go to fucking bed, Billy. Get up in the rack, turn your back, and look at the wall.

BILLY: You gotta be kiddin'.

ROGER: DO IT!

BILLY: Man . . . !

ROGER: Yeah . . . !

BILLY: You mean just . . .

ROGER: It been goin' on a long damn time, man. You ain't gonna put no stop to it.

CARLYLE: You . . . ain't . . . serious.

RICHIE (*both he and* CARLYLE *are staring at* ROGER *and then* BILLY, *who is staring at* ROGER): Well, I don't believe it. Of all the childish . . . infantile . . .

CARLYLE: Hey! (*Silence.*) HEY! Even I got to say this is a little weird, but if this the way you do it . . . (*And he turns toward* RICHIE *below him.*) . . . it the way I do it. I don't know.

RICHIE: With them right there? Are you kidding? My God, Carlyle, that'd be obscene. (*Pulling slightly away from* CARLYLE.)

CARLYLE: Ohhh, man . . . they backs turned.

RICHIE: No.

CARLYLE: What I'm gonna do? (*Silence. He looks at them, all three of them.*) Don't you got no feelin' for how a man feel? I don't understand you two boys. Unless'n you a pair of motherfuckers. That what you are, you a pair of motherfuckers? You slits, man. DON'T YOU HEAR ME!? I DON'T UNDERSTAND THIS SITUATION HERE. I THOUGHT WE MADE A DEAL!

(RICHIE *rises, starts to pull on his trousers.* CARLYLE *grabs him.*)

YOU GET ON YOUR KNEES, YOU PUNK, I MEAN NOW, AND YOU GONNA BE ON MY JOINT FAST OR YOU GONNA BE ONE BUSTED PUNK. AM I UNDERSTOOD? (*He hurls* RICHIE *down to the floor.*)

BILLY: I ain't gonna have this going on here; Roger, I can't.

ROGER: I been turnin' my back on one thing or another all my life.

RICHIE: Jealous, Billy?

BILLY (*getting to his feet*): Just go out that door, the two of you. Go. Go on out in the bushes or out in some field. See if I follow you. See if I care. I'll be right here and I'll be sleepin', but it ain't gonna be done in my house. I don't have much in this goddamn army, but HERE is mine. (*He stands beside his bed.*)

CARLYLE: I WANT MY FUCKIN' NUT! HOW COME YOU SO UPTIGHT? HE WANTS ME! THIS BOY HERE WANTS ME! WHO YOU TO STOP IT?

ROGER (*spinning to face* CARLYLE *and* RICHIE): THAT'S RIGHT, Billy. Richie one a those people want to get fucked by niggers, man. It what he know was gonna happen all his life—can be his dream come true. Ain't that right, Richie!

(*Jumping to his feet,* RICHIE *starts putting on his trousers.*)

Want to make it real in the world, how a nigger is an animal. Give 'em an inch, gonna take a mile. Ain't you some kinda fool, Richie? Hear me, Carlyle.

CARLYLE: Man, don't make me no nevermind what he think he's provin' an' shit, long as I get my nut. I KNOW I ain't no animal, don't have to prove it.

RICHIE (*pulling at Carlyle's arm, wanting to move him toward the door*): Let's go. Let's go outside. The hell with it.

(*But* CARLYLE *tears himself free; he squats furiously down on the bunk, his hands seizing it, his back to all of them.*)

CARLYLE: Bull shit. Bullshit! I ain't goin' no-fuckin'-where—this jive ass ain't runnin' me. Is this you house or not? (*He doesn't know what is going on; he can hardly look at any of them.*)

ROGER (*bounding out of bed, hurling his pillow across the room*): I'm goin' to the fuckin' john, Billy. Hang it up, man; let 'em be.

BILLY: No.

ROGER: I'm smarter than you—do like I'm sayin'.

BILLY: It ain't right.

ROGER: Who gives a big rat's ass!

CARLYLE: Right on, bro! That boy know; he do. (*He circles the bed toward them.*) Hear him. Look into his eyes.

BILLY: This fuckin' army takin' everything else away from me, they ain't takin' more than they got. I see what I see—I don't run, don't hide.

ROGER (*turning away from* BILLY, *stomps out the door, slamming it*): You fuckin' well better learn.

CARLYLE: That right. Time for more schoolin'. Lesson number one. (*Stealthily he steps and snaps out the only light, the lamp clamped to Richie's bed.*) You don't see what you see so well in the dark. It dark in the night. Black man got a black body—he disappear.

(*The darkness is so total, they are all no more than shadows.*)

RICHIE: Not to the hands; not to the fingers. (*Moving from across the room toward* CARLYLE.)

CARLYLE: You do like you talk, boy, you gonna make me happy.

(*As* BILLY, *nervously clutching his sneaker, is moving backward.*)

BILLY: Who says the lights go out? Nobody goddamn asked me if the lights go out.

(BILLY, *lunging to the wall switch, throws it. The overhead lights flash on, flooding the room with light.* CARLYLE *is seated on the edge of Richie's bed,* RICHIE *kneeling before him.*)

CARLYLE: I DO, MOTHERFUCKER, I SAY! (*And the switchblade seems to leap from his pocket to his hand.*) I SAY! CAN'T YOU LET PEOPLE BE?

(BILLY *hurls his sneaker at the floor at Carlyle's feet. Instantly* CAR-LYLE *is across the room, blocking Billy's escape out the door.*)

Goddamn you, boy! I'm gonna cut your ass, just to show you how it feel—and cuttin' can happen. This knife true.

RICHIE: Carlyle, now c'mon.

CARLYLE: Shut up, pussy.

RICHIE: Don't hurt him, for chrissake.

CARLYLE: Goddamn man throw a shoe at me, he don't walk around clean in the world thinkin' he can throw another. He get some shit come back at him.

(BILLY *doesn't know which way to go, and then* CARLYLE, *jabbing the knife at the air before Billy's chest, has* BILLY *running backward, his eyes fixed on the moving blade. He stumbles, having run into Richie's bed. He sprawls backward and* CARLYLE *is over him.*)

No, no; no, no. Put you hand out there. Put it out. (*Slight pause;* BILLY *is terrified.*) DO THE THING I'M TELLIN'!

(BILLY *lets his hand rise in the air and* CARLYLE *grabs it, holds it.*)

That's it. That's good. See? See?

(*The knife flashes across Billy's palm; the blood flows.* BILLY *winces, recoils, but Carlyle's hand still clenches and holds.*)

BILLY: Motherfucker.

(*Again the knife darts, cutting, and* BILLY *yelps.* RICHIE, *on his knees beside them, turns away.*)

RICHIE: Oh, my God, what are you—

CARLYLE (*in his own sudden distress, he flings the hand away*): That you blood. The blood inside you, you don't ever see it there. Take a look how easy it come out—and enough of it come out, you in the middle of the worst goddamn trouble you ever gonna see. And know I'm the man can deal that kinda trouble, easy as I smile. And I smile . . . easy. Yeah.

(BILLY *is curled in upon himself, holding the hand to his stomach as* RICHIE *now reaches tentatively and shyly out as if to console* BILLY, *who repulses the gesture.* CARLYLE *is angry and strangely depressed. Forlornly he slumps onto Billy's footlocker as* BILLY *staggers up to his wall locker and takes out a towel.*)

Bastard ruin my mood, Richie. He ruin my mood. Fightin' and lovin' real different in the feelin's I got. I see blood come outa somebody like that, it don't make me feel good—hurt me—hurt on somebody I thought was my friend. But I ain't supposed to see. One dumb nigger. No mind, he thinks, no heart, no feelings a gentleness. You see how that ain't true, Richie. Goddamn man threw a shoe at me. A lotta people woulda cut his heart out. I gotta make him know he throw shit, he get shit. But I don't hurt him bad, you see what I mean?

(*Billy's back is to them, as he stands hunched at his locker, and suddenly his voice, hissing, erupts.*)

BILLY: Jesus . . . H. . . . Christ . . . ! Do you know what I'm doin'? Do you know what I'm standin' here doin'? (*He whirls now; he holds a straight razor in his hand. A bloody towel is wrapped around the hurt hand.* CARLYLE *tenses, rises, seeing the razor.*) I'm a twenty-four-year-old goddamn college graduate—intellectual goddamn scholar type—and I got a razor in my hand. I'm thinkin' about comin' up behind one black human being and I'm thinkin' nigger this and nigger that—I wanna cut his throat. THAT IS RIDICULOUS. I NEVER FACED ANYBODY IN MY LIFE WITH ANYTHING TO KILL THEM. YOU UNDERSTAND ME? I DON'T HAVE A GODDAMN THING ON THE LINE HERE!

(*The door opens and* ROGER *rushes in, having heard the yelling.* BILLY *flings the razor into his locker.*)

Look at me, Roger, look at me. I got a cut palm—I don't know what happened. Jesus Christ, I got sweat all over me when I think a what I was near to doin'. I swear it. I mean, do I think I need a reputation as a killer, a bad man with a knife? (*He is wild with the energy of feeling free and with the anger at what these others almost made him do.* CARLYLE *slumps down on the footlocker; he sits there.*) Bullshit! I need shit! I got sweat all over me. I got the mile record in my hometown. I did four forty-two in high school, and that's the goddamn record in Windsor County. I don't need approval from either one of the pair of you. (*And he rushes at* RICHIE.) You wanna be a goddamn swish—a goddamn faggot-queer—GO! Suckin' cocks and takin' it in the ass, the thing of which you dream—GO! AND YOU— (*Whirling on* CARLYLE.) You wanna be a bad-assed animal, man, get it on—go—but I wash my hands. I am not human as you are. I put you down, I put you down— (*he almost hurls himself at* RICHIE)—you gay little piece a shit cake—SHIT CAKE. AND YOU— (*hurt, confused,* RICHIE *turns away, nearly pressing his face into the bed beside which he kneels, as* BILLY *has spun back to tower over the pulsing, weary* CARLYLE)—you are your own goddamn fault, SAMBO! SAMBO!

(*And the knife flashes up in Carlyle's hand into Billy's stomach, and* BILLY *yelps.*)

Ahhhhhhhhh. (*And pushes at the hand.* RICHIE *is still turned away.*)

RICHIE: Well, fuck you, Billy.
BILLY (*backs off the knife*): Get away, get away.
RICHIE (*as* ROGER, *who could not see because Billy's back is to him, is approaching* CARLYLE, *and* BILLY *goes walking up toward the lockers as if he knows where he is going, as if he is going to go out the door and to a movie, his hands holding his belly*): You're so-o messed up.
ROGER (*to* CARLYLE): Man, what's the matter with you?
CARLYLE: Don't nobody talk that weird shit to me, you understand?
ROGER: You jive, man. That's all you do—jive!

(BILLY, *striding swiftly, walks flat into the wall lockers; he bounces, turns. They are all looking at him.*)

RICHIE: Billy! Oh, Billy!

(ROGER *looks at* RICHIE.)

BILLY: Ahhhhhhh. Ahhhhhhh.

(ROGER *looks at* CARLYLE, *as if he is about to scream, and beyond him,* BILLY *turns from the lockers, starts to walk again, now staggering and moving toward them.*)

RICHIE: I think . . . he stabbed him. I think Carlyle stabbed Billy. Roger!

(ROGER *whirls to go to* BILLY, *who is staggering downstage and angled away, hands clenched over his belly.*)

BILLY: Shut up! It's just a cut, it's just a cut. He cut my hand, he cut my gut. (*He collapses onto his knees just beyond Roger's footlocker.*) It took the wind out of me, scared me, that's all. (*Fiercely he tries to hide the wound and remain calm.*)
ROGER: Man, are you all right?

(*He moves to* BILLY, *who turns to hide the wound. Till now no one is sure what happened.* RICHIE *only "thinks"* BILLY *has been stabbed.* BILLY *is pretending he isn't hurt. As* BILLY *turns from* ROGER, *he turns toward* RICHIE *and* RICHIE *sees the blood.* RICHIE *yelps and they all begin talking and yelling simultaneously.*)

CARLYLE (*overlapping*): You know what I was learnin', he was learnin' to talk all that weird shit, cuttin', baby, cuttin', the ways and means a shit, man, razors.
ROGER (*overlapping*): You all right? Or what? He slit you?
BILLY (*overlapping*): Just took the wind outa me, scared me.
RICHIE: Carlyle, you stabbed him; you stabbed him.
CARLYLE: Ohhhh, pussy, pussy, pussy, Carlyle know what he do.
ROGER (*trying to lift* BILLY): Get up, okay? Get up on the bed.
BILLY (*irritated, pulling free*): I am on the bed.
ROGER: What?
RICHIE: No, Billy, no, you're not.
BILLY: Shut up!
RICHIE: You're on the floor.

BILLY: I'm on the bed. I'm on the bed. (*Emphatically. And then he looks at the floor.*) What?

ROGER: Let me see what he did.

(*Billy's hands are clenched on the wound.*)

Billy, let me see where he got you.

BILLY (*recoiling*): NO–O–O–O–O–O, you nigger!

ROGER (*leaps at* CARLYLE): What did you do?

CARLYLE (*hunching his shoulders, ducking his head*): Shut up.

ROGER: What did you do, nigger—you slit him or stick him? (*And then he tries to get back to* BILLY.) Billy, let me see.

BILLY (*doubling over till his head hits the floor*): NO–O–O–O–O–O! Shit, shit, shit.

RICHIE (*suddenly sobbing and yelling*): Oh, my God, my God, ohhhh, ohhhh, ohhhh. (*Bouncing on his knees on the bed.*)

CARLYLE: FUCK IT, FUCK IT, I STUCK HIM. I TURNED IT. This mother army break my heart. I can't be out there where it pretty, don't wanna live! Wash me clean, shit face!

RICHIE: Ohhhh, ohhhhh, ohhhhhhhhhhh. Carlyle stabbed Billy, oh, ohhhh, I never saw such a thing in my life. Ohhhhhh.

(*As* ROGER *is trying gently, fearfully, to straighten* BILLY *up.*)

Don't die, Billy; don't die.

ROGER: Shut up and go find somebody to help. Richie, go!

RICHIE: Who? I'll go, I'll go. (*Scrambling off the bed.*)

ROGER: I don't know. JESUS CHRIST! DO IT!

RICHIE: Okay. Okay. Billy, don't die. Don't die. (*Backing for the door, he turns and runs.*)

ROGER: The sarge, or C.Q.

BILLY (*suddenly doubling over, vomiting blood;* RICHIE *is gone*): Ohhhhhhhhhh. Blood. Blood.

ROGER: Be still, be still.

BILLY (*pulling at a blanket on the floor beside him*): I want to stand up. I'm—vomiting— (*making no move to stand, only to cover himself*)—blood. What does that mean?

ROGER (*slowly standing*): I don't know.

BILLY: Yes, yes, I want to stand up. Give me blanket, blanket. (*He rolls back and forth, fighting to get the blanket over him.*)

ROGER: RIICCHHHIIIEEEE!

(*As* BILLY *is furiously grappling with the blanket.*)

No, no. (*He looks at* CARLYLE, *who is slumped over, muttering to himself. He runs for the door.*) Wait on, be tight, be cool.

BILLY: Cover me. Cover me.

(*At last he gets the blanket over his face. The dark makes him grow still. He lies there beneath his blanket. Silence. No one moves. And then* CARLYLE *senses the quiet; he turns, looks. Slowly, wearily, he rises and walks to where* BILLY *lies. He stands over him, the knife hanging loosely from his left hand as he reaches with his right to gently take the blanket and lift it slowly from Billy's face. They look at each other.* BILLY *reaches up and pats Carlyle's hand holding the blanket.*)

I don't want to talk to you right now, Carlyle. All right? Where's Roger? Do you know where he is? (*Slight pause.*) Don't stab me anymore, Carlyle, okay? I was dead wrong doin' what I did. I know that now. Carlyle, promise me you won't stab me anymore. I couldn't take it. Okay? I'm cold . . . my blood . . . is . . .

(*From off comes a voice.*)

ROONEY: Cokesy? Cokesy wokesy? (*And he staggers into the doorway, very drunk, a beer bottle in his hand.*) Ollie-ollie oxen-freeee. (*He looks at them.* CARLYLE *quickly, secretly, slips the knife into his pocket.*) How you all doin'? Everybody drunk, huh? I los' my friend. (*He is staggering sideways toward Billy's bunk, where he finally drops down, sitting.*) Who are you, soldier?

(CARLYLE *has straightened, his head ducked down as he is edging for the door.*)

Who are you, soldier?

(*And* RICHIE, *running, comes roaring into the room. He looks at* ROONEY *and cannot understand what is going on.* CARLYLE *is standing.* ROONEY *is just sitting there. What is going on?* RICHIE *moves along the lockers, trying to get behind* ROONEY, *his eyes never off* CARLYLE.)

RICHIE: Ohhhhhh, Sergeant Rooney, I've been looking for you everywhere—where have you been? Carlyle stabbed Billy, he stabbed him.

ROONEY (*sitting there*): What?

RICHIE: Carlyle stabbed Billy.

ROONEY: Who's Carlyle?

RICHIE: He's Carlyle.

(*As* CARLYLE *seems about to advance, the knife again showing in his hand*)

Carlyle, don't hurt anybody more!

ROONEY (*on his feet, he is staggering toward the door*): You got a knife there? What's with the knife? What's goin' on here?

(CARLYLE *steps as if to bolt for the door, but* ROONEY *is in the way, having inserted himself between* CARLYLE *and* RICHIE, *who has backed into the doorway.*)

Wait! Now wait!

RICHIE (*as* CARLYLE *raises the knife*): Carlyle, don't!

(*He runs from the room.*)

ROONEY: You watch your step, you understand. You see what I got here? (*He lifts the beer bottle, waves it threateningly.*) You watch your step, motherfucker. Relax. I mean, we can straighten all this out. We—

(CARLYLE *lunges at* ROONEY, *who tenses.*)

I'm just askin' what's goin' on, that's all I'm doin'. No need to get all—

(*And* CARLYLE *swipes at the air again;* ROONEY *recoils.*) Motherfucker. Motherfucker. (*He seems to be tensing, his body gathering itself for some mighty effort. And he throws his head back and gives the eagle yell.*) Eeeeeeeeeeeaaaaaaaaaaaaaaaahhhhhh! Eeeeaaaaaaaaaaaaahhhhhhhhhhhhh!

(CARLYLE *jumps; he looks left and right.*)

Goddammit, I'll cut you good. (*He lunges to break the bottle on the edge of the wall lockers. The bottle shatters and he yelps, dropping everything.*) Ohhhhhhhh! Ohhhhhhhhhhhhhh!

(CARLYLE *bolts, running from the room.*)

I hurt myself, I cut myself. I hurt my hand. (*Holding the wounded hand, he scurries to Billy's bed, where he sits on the edge, trying to wipe the blood away so he can see the wound.*) I cut—

(*Hearing a noise, he whirls, looks;* CARLYLE *is plummeting in the door and toward him.* ROONEY *stands.*)

I hurt my hand, goddammit!

(*The knife goes into Rooney's belly. He flails at* CARLYLE.)

I HURT MY HAND! WHAT ARE YOU DOING? WHAT ARE YOU DOING? WAIT! WAIT! (*He turns away, falling to his knees, and the knife goes into him again and again.*) No fair. No fair!

(ROGER, *running, skids into the room, headed for* BILLY, *and then he sees* CARLYLE *on* ROONEY, *the leaping knife.* ROGER *lunges, grabbing* CARLYLE, *pulling him to get him off* ROONEY. CARLYLE *leaps free of* ROGER, *sending* ROGER *flying backward. And then* CARLYLE *begins to circle Roger's bed. He is whimpering, wiping at the blood on his shirt as if to wipe it away.* ROGER *backs away as* CARLYLE *keeps waving the knife at him.* ROONEY *is crawling along the floor under Billy's bed and then he stops crawling, lies there.*)

CARLYLE: You don't tell nobody on me you saw me do this, I let you go, okay? Ohhhhhhhhh. (*Rubbing, rubbing at the shirt.*) Ohhhhhh, how'm I gonna get back to the world now, I got all this mess to—

ROGER: What happened? That you—I don't understand that you did this! That you did—

CARLYLE: YOU SHUT UP! Don't be talkin' all that weird shit to me—don't you go talkin' all that weird shit!

ROGER: Noooooooooooooo!

CARLYLE: I'm Carlyle, man. You know me. You know me.

(*He turns, he flees out the door.* ROGER, *alone, looks about the room.* BILLY *is there.* ROGER *moves toward* BILLY, *who is shifting, undulating on his back.*)

BILLY: Carlyle, no; oh, Christ, don't stab me anymore. I'll die. I will—I'll die. Don't make me die. I'll get my dog after you. I'LL GET MY DOG AFTER YOU!

(ROGER *is saying,* "Oh, Billy, man, Billy." *He is trying to hold* BILLY. *Now he lifts* BILLY *into his arms.*)

ROGER: Oh, Billy; oh, man. GODDAMMIT, BILLY!

(*As a* MILITARY POLICE LIEUTENANT *comes running in the door, his .45 automatic drawn, and he levels it at* ROGER.)

LIEUTENANT: Freeze, soldier! Not a quick move out of you. Just real slow, straighten your ass up.

(ROGER *has gone rigid; the* LIEUTENANT *is advancing on him. Tentatively,* ROGER *turns, looks.*)

ROGER: Huh? No.
LIEUTENANT: Get your ass against the lockers.
ROGER: Sir, no. I—
LIEUTENANT (*hurling* ROGER *away toward the wall lockers*): MOVE!

(*As another M.P.,* PFC HINSON, *comes in, followed by* RICHIE, *flushed and breathless.*)

Hinson, cover this bastard.

HINSON (*drawing his .45 automatic, moving on* ROGER): Yes, sir.

(*The* LIEUTENANT *frisks* ROGER, *who is spread-eagled at the lockers.*)

RICHIE: What? Oh, sir, no, no. Roger, what's going on?
LIEUTENANT: I'll straighten this shit out.
ROGER: Tell 'em to get the gun off me, Richie.
LIEUTENANT: SHUT UP!
RICHIE: But, sir, sir, he didn't do it. Not him.
LIEUTENANT (*fiercely he shoves* RICHIE *out of the way*): I told you,

all of you, to shut up. (*He moves to Rooney's body.*) Jesus, God, this Sfc is cut to shit. He's cut to shit. (*He hurries to Billy's body.*) This man is cut to shit.

(*As* CARLYLE *appears in the doorway, his hands cuffed behind him, a third M.P., PFC* CLARK, *shoving him forward.* CARLYLE *seems shocked and cunning, his mind whirring.*)

CLARK: Sir, I got this guy on the street, runnin' like a streak a shit.

(*He hurls the struggling* CARLYLE *forward and* CARLYLE *stumbles toward the head of Richie's bed as* RICHIE, *seeing him coming, hurries away along Billy's bed and toward the wall lockers.*)

RICHIE: He did it! Him, him!
CARLYLE: What is going on here? I don't know what is going on here!
CLARK (*club at the ready, he stations himself beside* CARLYLE): He's got blood all over him, sir. All over him.
LIEUTENANT: What about the knife?
CLARK: No, sir. He must have thrown it away.

(*As a fourth M.P. has entered to stand in the doorway, and* HINSON, *leaving* ROGER, *bends to examine* ROONEY. *He will also kneel and look for life in* BILLY.)

LIEUTENANT: You throw it away, soldier?
CARLYLE: Oh, you thinkin' about how my sister got happened, too. Oh, you ain't so smart as you think you are! No way!
ROGER: Jesus God almighty.
LIEUTENANT: What happened here? I want to know what happened here.
HINSON (*rising from Billy's body*): They're both dead, sir. Both of them.
LIEUTENANT (*confidential, almost whispering*): I know they're both dead. That's what I'm talkin' about.
CARLYLE: Chicken blood, sir. Chicken blood and chicken hearts is what all over me. I was goin' on my way, these people jump out the bushes be pourin' it all over me. Chicken blood and chicken hearts. (*Thrusting his hands out at* CLARK.) You goin' take these cuffs off me, boy?

LIEUTENANT: Sit him down, Clark. Sit him down and shut him up.

CARLYLE: This my house, sir. This my goddamn house.

(CLARK *grabs him, begins to move him.*)

LIEUTENANT: I said to shut him up.

CLARK: Move it; move! (*Struggling to get* CARLYLE *over to Roger's footlocker as* HINSON *and the other M. P. exit*)

CARLYLE: I want these cuffs taken off my hands.

CLARK: You better do like you been told. You better sit and shut up!

CARLYLE: I'm gonna be thinkin' over here. I'm gonna be thinkin' it all over. I got plannin' to do. I'm gonna be thinkin' in my quietness; don't you be makin' no mistake.

(*He slumps over, muttering to himself.* HINSON *and the other M. P. return, carrying a stretcher. They cross to* BILLY, *chatting with each other about how to go about the lift. They will lift him; they will carry him out.*)

LIEUTENANT (*to* RICHIE): You're Wilson?

RICHIE: No, sir. (*Indicating* BILLY.) That's Wilson. I'm Douglas.

LIEUTENANT (*to* ROGER): And you're Moore. And you sleep here.

ROGER: Yes, sir.

RICHIE: Yes, sir. And Billy slept here and Sergeant Rooney was our platoon sergeant and Carlyle was a transient, sir. He was a transient from P Company.

LIEUTENANT (*scrutinizing* ROGER): And you had nothing to do with this? (*To* RICHIE): He had nothing to do with this?

ROGER: No, sir, I didn't.

RICHIE: No, sir, he didn't. I didn't either. Carlyle went crazy and he got into a fight and it was awful. I didn't even know what it was about exactly.

LIEUTENANT: How'd the Sfc get involved?

RICHIE: Well, he came in, sir.

ROGER: I had to run off to call you, sir. I wasn't here.

RICHIE: Sergeant Rooney just came in—I don't know why—he heard all the yelling, I guess—and Carlyle went after him. Billy was already stabbed.

CARLYLE (*rising, his manner that of a man who is taking charge*): All right now, you gotta be gettin' the fuck outa here. All of you. I have decided enough of the shit has been goin' on around here and I am tellin' you to be gettin' these motherfuckin' cuffs off me and you be gettin' me a bus ticket home. I am quittin' this jive-time army.

LIEUTENANT: You are doin' what?

CARLYLE: No, I ain't gonna be quiet. No way. I am quittin' this goddamn—

LIEUTENANT: You shut the hell up, soldier. I am ordering you.

CARLYLE: I don't understand you people! Don't you people understand when a man be talkin' English at you to say his mind? I have quit the army!

(HINSON *returns.*)

LIEUTENANT: Get him outa here!

RICHIE: What's the matter with him?

LIEUTENANT: Hinson! Clark!

(*They move, grabbing* CARLYLE, *and they drag him, struggling, toward the door.*)

CARLYLE: Oh, no. Oh, no. You ain't gonna be doin' me no more. I been tellin' you. To get away from me. I am stayin' here. This my place, not your place. You take these cuffs off me like I been tellin' you! My poor little sister Lin Sue understood what was goin' on here! She tole me! She knew! (*He is howling in the hallway now.*) You better be gettin' these cuffs off me!

(*Silence.* ROGER, RICHIE, *and the* LIEUTENANT *are all staring at the door. The* LIEUTENANT *turns, crosses to the foot of Roger's bed.*)

LIEUTENANT: All right now. I will be getting to the bottom of this. You know I will be getting to the bottom of this. (*He is taking two forms from his clipboard.*)

RICHIE: Yes, sir.

(HINSON *and the fourth M.P. return with another stretcher. They walk to* ROONEY, *talking to one another about how to lift him. They drag him from under the bed. They will roll him onto the stretcher, lift him and walk out.* ROGER *moves, watching them, down along the edge of Billy's bed.*)

LIEUTENANT: Fill out these forms. I want your serial number, rank, your MOS, the NCOIC of your work. Any leave coming up will be canceled. Tomorrow at 0800 you will report to my office at the provost marshal's headquarters. You know where that is?

ROGER (*as the two M.P.'s are leaving with the stretcher and Rooney's body*): Yes, sir.

RICHIE: Yes, sir.

LIEUTENANT (*crossing to* ROGER, *he hands him two cards*):Be prepared to do some talking. Two perfectly trained and primed strong pieces of U.S. Army property got cut to shit up here. We are going to find out how and why. Is that clear?

RICHIE: Yes, sir.

ROGER: Yes, sir.

(*The* LIEUTENANT *looks at each of them. He surveys the room. He marches out.*)

RICHIE: Oh, my God. Oh. Oh.

(*He runs to his bed and collapses, sitting hunched down at the foot. He holds himself and rocks as if very cold.* ROGER, *quietly, is weeping. He stands and then walks to his bed. He puts down the two cards. He moves purposefully up to the mops hanging on the wall in the corner. He takes one down. He moves with the mop and the bucket to Billy's bed, where Rooney's blood stains the floor. He mops.* RICHIE, *in horror, is watching.*)

RICHIE: What . . . are you doing?

ROGER: This area a mess, man.

(*Dragging the bucket, carrying the mop, he moves to the spot where* BILLY *had lain. He begins to mop.*)

RICHIE: That's Billy's blood, Roger. His blood.

ROGER: Is it?

RICHIE: I feel awful.

ROGER (*keeps mopping*): How come you made me waste all that time talkin' shit to you, Richie? All my time talkin' shit, and all the time you was a faggot, man; you really was. You shoulda jus' tole ole Roger. He don't care. All you gotta do is tell me.

RICHIE: I've been telling you. I did.

ROGER: Jive, man, jive!

RICHIE: No!

ROGER: You did bullshit all over us! ALL OVER US!

RICHIE: I just wanted to hold his hand, Billy's hand, to talk to him, go to the movies hand in hand like he would with a girl or I would with someone back home.

ROGER: But he didn't wanna; HE didn't wanna.

(*Finished now,* ROGER *drags the mop and bucket back toward the corner.* RICHIE *is sobbing; he is at the edge of hysteria.*)

RICHIE: He did.

ROGER: No, man.

RICHIE: He did. He did. It's not my fault.

(ROGER *slams the bucket into the corner and rams the mop into the bucket. Furious, he marches down to* RICHIE. *Behind him* SER-GEANT COKES, *grinning and lifting a wine bottle, appears in the doorway.*)

COKES: Hey!

(RICHIE, *in despair, rolls onto his belly.* COKES *is very, very happy.*)

Hey! What a day, gen'l'men. How you all doin'?

ROGER (*crossing up near the head of his own bed*): Hello, Sergeant Cokes.

COKES (*affectionate and casual, he moves near to* ROGER): How you all doin'? Where's ole Rooney? I lost him.

ROGER: What?

COKES: We had a hell of a day, ole Rooney and me, lemme tell you. We been playin' hide-and-go-seek, and I was hidin', and now I think maybe he started hidin' without tellin' me he was gonna and I can't find him and I thought maybe he was hidin' up here.

RICHIE: Sergeant, he—

ROGER: No. No, we ain't seen him.

COKES: I gotta find him. He knows how to react in a tough situation. He didn't come up here looking for me?

(ROGER *moves around to the far side of his bed, turning his back to* COKES. *Sitting,* ROGER *takes out a cigarette, but he does not light it.*)

ROGER: We was goin' to sleep, Sarge. Got to get up early. You know the way this mother army is.

COKES (*nodding, drifting backward, he sits down on Billy's bed*): You don't mind I sit here a little. Wait on him. Got a little wine. You can have some. (*Tilting his head way back, he takes a big drink and then, looking straight ahead, corks the bottle with a whack of his hand.*) We got back into the area—we had been downtown—he wanted to play hide-and-go-seek. I tole him okay, I was ready for that. He hid his eyes. So I run and hid in the bushes and then under this Jeep. 'Cause I thought it was better. I hid and I hid and I hid. He never did come. So finally, I got tired—I figured I'd give up, come lookin' for him. I was way over by the movie theater. I don't know how I got there. Anyway, I got back here and I figured maybe he come up here lookin' for me, figurin' I was hidin' up with you guys. You ain't seen him, huh?

ROGER: No, we ain't seen him. I tole you that, Sarge.

COKES: Oh.

RICHIE: Roger!

ROGER: He's drunk, Richie! He's blasted drunk. Got a brain turned to mush!

COKES (*in deep agreement*): That ain't no lie.

ROGER: Let it be for the night, Richie. Let him be for the night.

COKES: I still know what's goin' on, though. Never no worry about that. I always know what's goin' on. I always know. Don't matter what I drink or how much I drink. I always still know what's goin' on. But . . . I'll be goin' maybe and look for Rooney. (*But rising, he wanders down center.*) But . . . I mean, we could be doin' that forever. Him and me. Me under the Jeep. He wants to find me, he goes to the Jeep. I'm over here. He comes here. I'm gone. You know, maybe I'll just wait a little while more I'm here. He'll find me then if he comes here. You guys want another drink? (*Turning, he goes to Billy's footlocker, where he sits and takes another enormous guzzle of wine.*) Jesus, what a goddamn day we had. Me and Rooney started drivin' and we was comin' to this intersection and out comes this goddamn Chevy. I try to get around her, but no dice. BINGO! I hit her in the left rear. She was furious. I didn't care. I gave her my name and number. My car had a headlight out, the fender bashed in. Rooney wouldn't stop laughin'. I didn't know what to do. So we went to D.C. to this private club I know. Had ten or more snorts and decided to get back here after playin' some snooker. That was fun. On the way, we picked up this kid from the engineering unit, hitchhiking. I'm starting to feel real clearheaded now. So I'm comin' around this corner and all of a sudden there's this car stopped dead in front of me. He's not blinkin' to turn or anything. I slam on the brakes, but it's like puddin' the way I slide into him. There's a big noise and we yell. Rooney starts laughin' like crazy and the kid jumps outa the back and says he's gonna take a fuckin' bus. The guy from the other car is swearin' at me. My car's still workin' fine, so I move it off to the side and tell him to do the same, while we wait for the cops. He says he wants his car right where it is and he had the right of way 'cause he was makin' a legal turn. So we're waitin' for the cops. Some cars go by. The guy's car is this big fuckin' Buick. Around the corner comes this little red Triumph. The driver's this blond kid got this blond girl next to him. You can see what's gonna happen. There's this fuckin' car sittin' there, nobody in it. So the Triumph goes crashin' into the back of the Buick with nobody in it. BIFF-BANG-BOOM. And everything stops. We're staring. It's all still. And then that fuckin' Buick kinda shudders and starts to move. With nobody in it. It starts to roll from the impact. And it rolls just far enough to get where the road starts a downgrade. It's driftin' to the right. It's driftin' to the shoulder and over it and onto this hill, where it's pickin' up speed 'cause the hill is steep and then it disappears over the side, and into the dark, just rollin' real quiet. Rooney falls over, he's laughin' so hard. I don't know what to do. In a minute the cops come and in another minute some guy comes runnin' up over the hill to tell us some other guy had got run over by this car with nobody in it. We didn't know what to think. This was fuckin' unbelievable to us. But we found out later from the cops that this wasn't true and some guy had got hit over the head with a bottle in a bar and when he staggered out the door it was just at the instant that this fuckin' Buick with nobody in it went by. Seein' this, the guy stops cold and turns around and just goes back into the bar. Rooney is screamin' at me how we been in four goddamn accidents and fights and how we have got out clean. So

then we got everything all straightened out and we come back
here to play hide-and-seek 'cause that's what ole Rooney wanted.
(*He is taking another drink, but finding the bottle empty.*) Only now I
can't find him.

(*Near Richie's footlocker stands a beer bottle, and* COKES *begins to
move toward it. Slowly he bends and grasps the bottle; he straightens,
looking at it. He drinks. And settles down on Richie's footlocker.*)

I'll just sit a little.

(RICHIE, *lying on his belly, shudders. The sobs burst out of him. He is
shaking.* COKES, *blinking, turns to study* RICHIE.)

What's up? Hey, what're you cryin' about, soldier? Hey?

(RICHIE *cannot help himself.*)

What's he cryin' about?

ROGER (*disgustedly, he sits there*): He's cryin' 'cause he's a queer.
COKES: Oh. You a queer, boy?
RICHIE: Yes, Sergeant.
COKES: Oh. (*Pause.*) How long you been a queer?
ROGER: All his fuckin' life.
RICHIE: I don't know.
COKES (*turning to scold* ROGER): Don't be yellin' mean at him. Boy,
I tell you it's a real strange thing the way havin' leukemia gives
you a lotta funny thoughts about things. Two months ago—or
maybe even yesterday—I'da called a boy who was a queer a lotta
awful names. But now I just wanna be figurin' things out. I
mean, you ain't kiddin' me out about ole Rooney, are you, boys,
'cause of how I'm a sergeant and you're enlisted men, so you got
some idea a vengeance on me? You ain't doin' that, are you, boys?
ROGER: No.
RICHIE: Ohhhh. Jesus. Ohhhh. I don't know what's hurtin' in me.
COKES: No, no, boy. You listen to me. You gonna be okay. There's a
lotta worse things in this world than bein' a queer. I seen a lot of
'em, too. I mean, you could have leukemia. That's worse. That
can kill you. I mean, it's okay. You listen to the ole sarge. I mean,
maybe I was a queer, I wouldn't have leukemia. Who's to say?

Lived a whole different life. Who's to say? I keep thinkin' there was maybe somethin' I coulda done different. Maybe not drunk so much. Or if I'd killed more gooks, or more krauts or more dinks. I was kindhearted sometimes. Or if I'd had a wife and I had some kids. Never had any. But my mother did and she died of it anyway. Gives you a whole funny different way a lookin' at things, I'll tell you. Ohhhhh, Rooney, Rooney. (*Slight pause.*) Or if I'd let that little gook outa that spider hole he was in, I was sittin' on it. I'd let him out now, he was in there. (*He rattles the footlocker lid under him.*) Oh, how'm I ever gonna forget it? That funny little guy. I'm runnin' along, he pops up outa that hole. I'm never gonna forget him—how'm I ever gonna forget him? I see him and dive, goddamn bullet hits me in the side, I'm midair, everything's turnin' around. I go over the edge of this ditch and I'm crawlin' real fast. I lost my rifle. Can't find it. Then I come up behind him. He's half out of the hole. I bang him on top of his head, stuff him back into the hole with a grenade for company. Then I'm sittin' on the lid and it's made outa steel. I can feel him in there, though, bangin' and yellin' under me, and his yelling I can hear is begging for me to let him out. It was like a goddamn Charlie Chaplin movie, everybody fallin' down and clumsy, and him in there yellin' and bangin' away, and I'm just sittin' there lookin' around. And he was Charlie Chaplin. I don't know who I was. And then he blew up. (*Pause.*) Maybe I'll just get a little shut-eye right sittin' here while I'm waitin' for ole Rooney. We figure it out. All of it. You don't mind I just doze a little here, you boys?

ROGER: No.

RICHIE: No.

(ROGER *rises and walks to the door. He switches off the light and gently closes the door. The transom glows.* COKES *sits in a flower of light.* ROGER *crosses back to his bunk and settles in, sitting.*)

COKES: Night, boys.

RICHIE: Night, Sergeant.

(COKES *sits there, fingers entwined, trying to sleep.*)

COKES: I mean, he was like Charlie Chaplin. And then he blew up.
ROGER (*suddenly feeling very sad for this old man*): Sergeant . . .
    maybe you was Charlie Chaplin, too.
COKES: No. No. (*Pause.*) No. I don't know who I was. Night.
ROGER: You think he was singin' it?
COKES: What?
ROGER: You think he was singin' it?
COKES: Oh, yeah. Oh, yeah; he was singin' it.

(*Slight pause.* COKES, *sitting on the footlocker, begins to sing a makeshift language imitating Korean, to the tune of "Beautiful Streamer." He begins with an angry, mocking energy that slowly becomes a dream, a lullaby, a farewell, a lament.*)

Yo no som lo no
Ung toe lo knee
Ra so me la lo
La see see oh doe.
Doe no tee ta ta
Too low see see
Ra mae me lo lo
Ah boo boo boo eee.
Boo boo eee booo eeee
La so lee lem
Lem lo lee da ung
Uhhh so ba booooo ohhhh.
Boo booo eee ung ba
Eee eee la looo
Lem lo lala la
Eeee oohhh ohhh ohhh ohhhhh.

(*In the silence, he makes the soft, whispering sound of a child imitating an explosion, and his entwined fingers come apart. The dark figures of* RICHIE *and* ROGER *are near. The lingering light fades to black.*)

Streamers was produced by the Long Wharf Theater on January 30, 1976, under the direction of Mike Nichols, with the following cast:

MARTIN	Michael-Raymond O'Keefe
RICHIE	Peter Evans
CARLYLE	Joe Fields
BILLY	John Heard
ROGER	Herbert Jefferson, Jr.
COKES	Dolph Sweet
ROONEY	Kenneth McMillan
M.P. LIEUTENANT	Stephen Mendillo
PFC HINSON (M.P.)	Ron Siebert
PFC CLARK (M.P.)	Michael Kell

Producer, Arvin Brown; set by Tony Walton; costumes by Bill Walker; lighting by Ronald Wallace; stage manager, Nina Seely.

Streamers was produced in New York by Joseph Papp on April 21, 1976, at the Mitzi Newhouse Theater, Lincoln Center, under the direction of Mike Nichols, with the following cast:

MARTIN	Michael Kell
RICHIE	Peter Evans
CARLYLE	Dorian Harewood
BILLY	Paul Rudd
ROGER	Terry Alexander
COKES	Dolph Sweet
ROONEY	Kenneth McMillan
M.P. LIEUTENANT	Arlen Dean Snyder
PFC HINSON (M.P.)	Les Roberts
PFC CLARK (M.P.)	Mark Metcalf
FOURTH M.P.	Miklos Horvath

Associate Producer, Bernard Gersten; set by Tony Walton; costumes by Bill Walker; lighting by Ronald Wallace; stage manager, Nina Seely.

The
Orphan

For the teachers and students of Villanova Theatre, 1967–1972

Let no one think for an instant that we, in our vaunted modern civilization, have gone "beyond the primitive human sacrifice."

—ROLLO MAY,
Power and Innocence

CHARACTERS

THE FIGURE

THE SPEAKER

ORESTES

CLYTEMNESTRA ONE

CLYTEMENSTRA TWO

AGAMEMNON

AEGISTHUS

THE GIRL

ELECTRA

IPHIGENIA

THE FAMILY MEMBERS:

PYLADES

BECKY

JENNY

SALLY

ACT ONE

Darkness: we hear a rhythmic breathing, an eerie rattle, and then the lights rise to show us: A large rope cargo net hangs vertically upstage. Behind it and stretching downstage on either side of the cargo net are a series of ramps and platforms with rope wound around the ramps, the railings, the struts, the beams, their texture echoing that of the net. The lights rise slowly and we see SALLY, BECKY, *and* JENNY *scattered about and seeming to sleep. With them is* PYLADES, *a young man in a dark jumpsuit. Eight white heads hang from the ceiling, a planetary swirl amid which other white fragments are strewn, as if a giant statue has broken apart.* CLYTEMNESTRA ONE *and* CLYTEMNESTRA TWO *sit behind the large hanging cargo net. They wear identical costumes, elegant silky gowns. They are the same person at two different points of time in her life.*

CLYTEMNESTRA TWO *is ten years older than* CLYTEMNESTRA ONE. *A single shawl is spread across their shoulders. One is young, thoughtful, hopeful; the other violent, sensual, bitter. Under the Stage Left scaffold stands* IPHIGENIA, *a girl dressed in white. Upstage and off to the side is* AGAMEMNON, *wearing a dark shirt, trousers, and dress shoes. On the top level of the scaffold stands* THE GIRL. *She wears a blouse and jeans and beads. Her feet are bare. Downstage is* THE FIGURE, *a man with a thick black beard; he wears a T-shirt, Levi's jacket and jeans, and boots. He is lean and agile. He has long dark hair but it is now tied up, or held in a ponytail. Beside him stands* THE SPEAKER, *a young woman dressed elegantly, a sexy satin gown, lush and form-fitting, her eyes closed as if she dozes on her feet; in her hands, hanging at her side, she holds a flashlight and a microphone.*

Now THE FIGURE *leans close to the Speaker's ear:*

THE FIGURE: Say "Good Evening."

THE SPEAKER (*eyes open as she speaks into her mike*): Good evening.

(As THE FIGURE *is retreating.*)

In a place like this we all begin. Deep within the dark of another's belly. The smallest and largest cells collide and multiplying ten thousand times possess one beating heart. Think of time as a pool. Do we speak to the past? Or merely look at it? Is it right? Left? Up? Down?

(*She shines her light in many directions, hitting* ORESTES *as he comes running in. He wears a T-shirt, trousers.*)

Here comes Orestes.

(BECKY *kisses him.*)

ORESTES: I have been told I am Orestes.
BECKY: It is written that you kill your mother.
THE FIGURE (*high in the scaffolding*): You want to kill your mother. You want Clytemnestra dead.
ORESTES: I have been told I kill my mother. I want some time to have my mother dead.

(As *he draws a sword from his belt,* ELECTRA *wanders across the stage.*)

THE SPEAKER: There is Electra.

(ORESTES *moves toward her, and she seems to flee him. He is grabbed and spun by* JENNY. *Other* FAMILY MEMBERS *push him.*)

CLYTEMNESTRA ONE: And all is mist.
CLYTEMNESTRA TWO: When there is a thing that I must touch, I reach.

(*They strain forward against the net.*)

CLYTEMNESTRA ONE: I am dirt.
CLYTEMNESTRA TWO: It flees.
THE SPEAKER: She is as you see, One and Two. Ten years older. Ten years younger.

(*The Speaker's flashlight hits each of them.*)

Clytemnestra. Clytemnestra.

CLYTEMNESTRA ONE: I—
CLYTEMNESTRA TWO: I—

(*They rise and spin off from one another, whirling in opposite directions.*)

THE SPEAKER: She splits like an atom. Divides like a cell. Multiplying into the future.

THE FIGURE (*high in the scaffolding*): And all is like a strange impossible Monday when you must kill and kill your mother.

ORESTES: And all is like a strange impossible Monday when I must kill . . . and kill my mother.

(ORESTES *moves toward* CLYTEMNESTRA ONE, *his sword pointing at her as she backs away in fear, and* BECKY *plucks the sword from his hand and gives it to someone else. Off the sword goes, passing from hand to hand across the space behind him as he stands there dazed, watching.*)

THE SPEAKER: Before the advent of the special theory of relativity—

BECKY: No one ever thought there could be any ambiguity in the statement—

SALLY: —that two events in different places happened at the same time—

JENNY: —or that two events in different places happened at different times—

THE SPEAKER AND FAMILY: Science found, however, that two events in different places may appear simultaneous to one observer—

BECKY: While another may judge that the second event preceded the first—

JENNY: —and still a third may say—

THE SPEAKER: —that the first event preceded the second.

SALLY: This would occur when the three observers were moving rapidly relative to one another.

THE SPEAKER: May this not also mean the opposite?

THE SPEAKER AND FAMILY (*as they spin off into new positions*): May it not be that events thought to be in sequence, are in fact, simultaneous?

(*And the sword is put back into the hand of* ORESTES.)

ORESTES: She fills the corners of my room. She fills the corners of my room.

(*Behind* ORESTES *fire flares.* AGAMEMNON *stands as he strides forward.*)

AGAMEMNON: Curious, how the smell of incense is sweeter than the bones of Troy burning. In this flickering, I see the way a face can change with fear or flame. I am tired. I am home. I have seen the sleeping face of my child.

(CLYTEMNESTRA TWO *is moving from behind the net to approach him.*)

CLYTEMNESTRA TWO: You shall bathe. We will bathe together.

(*He laughs warmly.*)

The tub is prepared with scented water. The sheets of our bed are fresh. Wine and fruit await us.

(*She sighs, touching him, as* AEGISTHUS *enters, wheeling out the tub. The tub is a laundry basket on wheels with a towel draped over the side.*)

Go to the tub.

AGAMEMNON: I will. And you will join me. (*Reaching to remove the strap of her dress.*) Who is the servant?

(AEGISTHUS *bows.*)

And my Trojan slave—the girl, Cassandra, my prize of war, where is she?

CLYTEMNESTRA TWO: I have sent her to the kitchens.
AGAMEMNON: It is said she knows the future.

(AEGISTHUS *smashes down a club upon the head of* AGAMEMNON, *who, crying out, falls to the floor.*)

CLYTEMNESTRA TWO: Whoring in your foreign bed, did she tell you of this moment in the future? Or of the moment only minutes ago, when her own throat was cut in the kitchens? Put him in the tub. He is important in the tub.

(AGAMEMNON *groans as they work to lift him.*)

You smell of time gone, Agamemnon. It's time that you bathe. Let it begin that you bathe. You are filth and filth must bathe.

(*They have dumped his slack body in the tub. Now she is looking about.*)

Where's the net? We must have the net.

AEGISTHUS: I see no net.

(AGAMEMNON *is stirring.*)

CLYTEMNESTRA TWO: He moves; already he starts to awaken. Where is the net? We must have the net and knife!

THE FIGURE: Clytemnestra! (*In the scaffolding high above them he stands, waving the net.*) Clytemnestra! . . .

AEGISTHUS: Who's that?

CLYTEMNESTRA TWO: He has the net.

AEGISTHUS: Who is it?

THE FIGURE: I have the net.

AEGISTHUS: It is Apollo!

CLYTEMNESTRA TWO: Apollo?

AEGISTHUS: Apollo, God of Reason, has the net. (*And slowly* THE FIGURE *is descending the ladder toward them.*) Born on the little island of Delos, he is a master musician, the God of Truth from whom no lie can come, the God of Light and reason in whom there is no dark at all.

THE FIGURE: Your thighs are white and perfect, Clytemnestra. What is he, Agamemnon, always poking and seeking in the air outside himself, his feeble seed desolate on sand or stone, till he can enter the rich earth of your belly. He rises into emptiness, stands obvious and simple. You are a clever, subtle cavern, deep and jeweled within.

CLYTEMNESTRA TWO: Apollo, am I chosen? Have you chosen me?

THE FIGURE: What other life have we but you? Clytemnestra, you are all. (*He has put the net around her shoulders. Now he is backing away from her.*) All!

CLYTEMNESTRA TWO: Oh, Apollo, no; I worship you.

THE FIGURE: I worship you.

CLYTEMNESTRA TWO: I have the net, Aegisthus!

(AEGISTHUS *reaches to take an end of the net.*)

Look, I have the net!

(*They move to spread the net above* AGAMEMNON *in the tub.*)

And when we drop the net upon him.

AEGISTHUS: We drop the net upon him.

CLYTEMNESTRA TWO: We drop the net upon him.

(*And they fling the net down upon* AGAMEMNON *and then leap backward.*)

AGAMEMNON (*slowly, carefully, a little perplexed, takes hold of the net*): What's this? What's this?

ORESTES (*rushing forward, raging, sword in hand*): She fills the corners of my room!

CLYTEMNESTRA ONE: I am—

CLYTEMNESTRA TWO: —dirt! (*This is with revulsion.*)

CLYTEMNESTRA ONE: Dirt!

(*And the telephone begins to ring loudly, spreading fear through everyone. They scurry back and forth, looking upward.*)

THE SPEAKER: We call to one another across space—our voices pass through distance—may we not call through time, also—down and up, let us say, through time.

IPHIGENIA: Hello. Hello.

THE SPEAKER: May we not also call through time.

ORESTES: Hello.

AGAMEMNON: Hello.

AEGISTHUS: Hello.

CLYTEMNESTRA ONE: Hello.

CLYTEMNESTRA TWO: Hello.

THE GIRL (*standing in a far corner of the scaffolding*): Well, I was just the kinda person who would groove, see, just flow with the moment. Because I knew society was not worthy of my respect, I made up my own, only my justice was just, unlike the regular one. I had this man offer to marry me and he was older so I fled, and shortly thereafter, on acid, I saw down into the center of the earth, and I said, "Oh, God, just take me now for yours." And the next day, I met this man . . .

(THE FIGURE *moves behind her to embrace her.*)

. . . and he sang for me and knew my heart and he was Abaddon, the angel, and I was in his Army.

(*The ringing stops.*)

CLYTEMNESTRA TWO (*moving sadly to* ORESTES, *who raises his sword as she moves on past him toward* CLYTEMNESTRA ONE): And now I see Orestes, and the thing I am seeking is a knife of silver in his fingers.

CLYTEMNESTRA ONE (*moving to sadly embrace* CLYTEMNESTRA TWO): Having fallen to him.

THE FIGURE: Through the flesh of the father to the hand of the son falls the sword.

(*And* ORESTES *has moved to stand beside* CLYTEMNESTRA ONE *and* TWO, *holding the sword pointed at them, as* ELECTRA *comes wandering by.*)

ELECTRA: I was so important, so important.

CLYTEMNESTRA ONE AND CLYTEMNESTRA TWO: Who will help us?

THE FIGURE: I am here.

PYLADES: Apollo is a God.

THE GIRL: Oh, wow.

AEGISTHUS: I was the most important person in the world and they killed me.

EVERYONE: What time is it? What time is it?

THE SPEAKER: It passes; goes by.

AEGISTHUS: Bubbles mark the ocean for a moment where we drown.

CLYTEMNESTRA ONE: I hold the infant of my son, Orestes, in my arms.

CLYTEMNESTRA TWO: I hold the infant of my killer in my arms.

(*Both are happy as they sit side by side, rocking invisible infants.*)

THE FIGURE: Keep your son an infant, she believes, and you will
   never die.
AEGISTHUS: What about Orestes?
THE SPEAKER: He kills you, Aegisthus.
CLYTEMNESTRA ONE: I don't.

(*They look at* AEGISTHUS, *then at each other.*)

CLYTEMNESTRA TWO: I don't.
THE SPEAKER: And you, Clytemnestra.
CLYTEMNESTRA TWO: Nooo.
CLYTEMNESTRA ONE: Nooo.
CLYTEMNESTRA TWO: I am not Agamemnon.
CLYTEMNESTRA ONE: I live.
AGAMEMNON (*reaching up in the tub, presses tentatively against the
   net*): I want to be Aegisthus!
THE SPEAKER: You are Agamemnon.
AEGISTHUS: I want to be Agamemnon.
THE SPEAKER: You are Aegisthus.
AGAMEMNON: What is this net? What is it? It smells of fish. I can
   smell the sea. (*Now he is struggling in the net.*) It holds me
   whatever way I go. What is this net? I'll tear the threads. I'll tear
   them. It doesn't tear. I'll rip them. I'll rip and tear. I'll bite them.
   I'll bite. They taste of salt. Fish and salt. I'll pull them off. I'll
   pull. (*Now his struggle is frantic.*) I'll bite them. Bite and throw.
   Bite it, throw it, tear it. It doesn't! It doesn't! I'll rip and tear!
   I'll— I'll— CASSANDRAAAAAAAAA! WHAT IS THIS NET?

THE SPEAKER (*walking up, shining the light on him in the tub*):
   He, Agamemnon, at one point, killed a young king and stole his
   wife. He killed their infant son and took the young queen to be
   his own, and she was Clytemnestra.

(*Flashlight on* CLYTEMNESTRA ONE, *who moves to kneel on the
floor in front of* AGAMEMNON, *who still struggles slowly, wearily in
the tub.*)

At another point, he Agamemnon . . .

(*Flashlight on* AGAMEMNON.)

sacrificed the life of his daughter, Iphigenia . . .

(*Flashlight on* IPHIGENIA *as she moves to kneel beside* CLYTEM-
NESTRA ONE, *putting her head into her mother's lap.*)

born of Clytemnestra in order that the wind would arise and
power his ships to Troy. At still another point, she . . .

(*Flashlight on* CLYTEMNESTRA TWO, *who moves to kneel beside*
CLYTEMNESTRA ONE.)

and he . . .

(*Flashlight on* AEGISTHUS, *who moves to stand behind the kneeling*
CLYTEMNESTRA TWO *and beside* AGAMEMNON.)

murdered him. They put down upon Agamemnon a fish net and
stabbed

(*Lights on* AGAMEMNON, *as* ORESTES *moves near, looking for a
place in this family portrait.*)

with a haunted knife of eight inches and imperfect alloy. And
she—

(*Flashlight on* THE GIRL. *They all look.*)

THE GIRL (*leaping to her feet and bounding down from one level to
the next, joyous, exuberant*): I mean, one a the things about great
Abaddon, our leader, that anybody woulda admired was how he
knew about people and he says, "Be kind to 'em; don't be tellin'
'em how you're gonna kill 'em. Let 'em go in peace into eternity,"
he says. 'Cause the last thing you're doin' when you die, you just
keep doin' it—just, oh, wow, screamin' the whole way a eternity.
IPHIGENIA: He makes me think of dogs. They lick my breasts. They
suck my tongue. He fills my sweating brain with dogs. I do not
know I die. Iphigenia does not know she dies. What is his name?

(*And behind her* THE FIGURE *is moving toward her. He wears a toga
woven with bones over the white T-shirt; he wears a bone necklace and
a half-mask molded to the contours of his own face.*)

AEGISTHUS (*hurrying downstage with a portfolio from which he pulls various items*): I have maps that show all we own. They indicate the length and breadth of things, the up and down, this and that; they show the top and bottom, both sides, trees and ocean.

THE FIGURE (*grabs* IPHIGENIA *from behind*): Calchas! Calchas! Mask of God made manifest in man, Priest, and prophet.

AGAMEMNON: I kill a thousand Trojans.

CLYTEMNESTRA TWO: I kill Agamemnon.

CLYTEMNESTRA ONE: I kill a man; a husband.

AGAMEMNON: I kill a daughter.

ORESTES: I kill my mother.

(*There is a curious note of music. The characters are spread about the stage.* IPHIGENIA *is near her father.* CLYTEMNESTRA ONE *is beside her husband.* CLYTEMNESTRA TWO *is between* AEGISTHUS *and* AGAMEMNON. ORESTES *is alone. The music rises and together they all sing, except for* THE SPEAKER *who moves about observing.*)

All:
The sand in an hourglass, measuring time, is
more or less accurate,
which is to say, more or less inaccurate.
We say "Monday," we say "Tuesday.
I must do this, I must do that
Help, hello, I drown, I drown."
We say "Monday," we say "Tuesday.
I must do this, I must do that,
Help, hello, I drown, I drown."
The sand in an hourglass, measuring time, is
more or less accurate,
which is to say, more or less inaccurate.

Bubbles mark the ocean for a moment where we
drown.
Bubbles mark the ocean for a moment where we
drown.
Bubbles mark the ocean for a moment where we
drown.
Bubbles mark the ocean for a moment where we
drown.

THE SPEAKER (*as all are exiting*): They come and go; there have been the Greeks and Romans, the Serbs and Greco-Romans; there have been the Croatians, the Chinese, the Assyrians, Arabs, Jews. Today there are the Arabs, Russians, Jews, the Americans, Arabs, Chinese, Serbs, Croatians and Japanese and others.

(*It has been a spinning of activity, all leaving,* BECKY *handing* AGAMEMNON *a message as he climbs from the tub and* THE FIGURE *puts on the mask of Calchas and they are priest and king.*)

THE FIGURE: It is my burden to know what I know, Agamemnon. You must do as I say.

AGAMEMNON: No.

THE FIGURE: You must send for your daughter.

AGAMEMNON (*angrily turning to face Calchas*): I should have been told of your plan before you spoke at council. There is no time now. Think of the weeks as she travels; the wind could come before she arrived and we would seem foolish.

THE FIGURE: Artemis has dreamed in lust of your child.

AGAMEMNON: The Goddess said this to you, used the name of Iphigenia, spoke my name?

THE FIGURE: They confer about you, Agamemnon. They analyze your thoughts, discuss your deeds. All you do is written in scrolls of smoke they read and murmur about among themselves.

AGAMEMNON: I please the Gods; I pay them homage.

THE FIGURE: But only with your words. Let your deeds obey the Gods, or by your own example, you will teach mutiny to the army you want to rule.

AGAMEMNON: We are chained to this place, Priest! The most powerful army in the world.

THE FIGURE: And Iphigenia is the key. In smoke and the moon and the innards of a blessed and God-sent bird, I have read Iphigenia must die.

AGAMEMNON: Why do I not hear them? It is my daughter.

THE FIGURE: I feel in my pulse the movement of each star. Am I not the priest of Apollo? Apollo made manifest in man, the issue of wisdom begotten by knowledge! (*Pause.*) Send for the child. The wind must have her.

AGAMEMNON: What am I to say to her? "Come, my child. Journey to us so that we may kill you."

THE FIGURE: No, no, lie to her. Trick her. Write a letter. Send the letter now. (*He hands a scroll to* AGAMEMNON.) Pray to God Apollo if you have need.

(*As a servant runs up and snatches the scroll from* AGAMEMNON, *and running off the* SERVANT *hands the note to* BECKY, *who puts it in an envelope and crosses away with it.*)

Pray. God is here. Call out to him. Call to Apollo. God is good.

(THE FIGURE *is leaving as* JENNY *takes the letter from* BECKY. AGAMEMNON *is following after* THE FIGURE, *the letter passing from the hands of* JENNY *to those of* SALLY.)

AGAMEMNON: I will beg her not to die. I will beg the knife not to kill her—her skin not to open, her heart to go on beating, though you, Priest, hold it in your hand. She is my child! Iphigenia!

IPHIGENIA: Who calls me? Who calls? Hello.

(*High in the scaffolding, she stands, having heard her name. She looks about and starts climbing down as still the letter travels from one person to another across the space and* CLYTEMNESTRA ONE *stands behind the cargo net, waiting.*)

THE SPEAKER: Sound consists of waves that need air to travel. Sounds wiggle through the fabric of the air. Experimenters have sent out signals and gotten back echoes from two million miles beyond the moon.

IPHIGENIA: What does the letter say, Mother?

(CLYTEMNESTRA ONE, *reading the letter, looks up in surprise to see both* IPHIGENIA *and* ELECTRA.)

You have a letter. May I know what it says?

CLYTEMNESTRA ONE: This and that. It says this and that. (*She turns away from them.*)

IPHIGENIA: I know it's from Father.

(IPHIGENIA *and* ELECTRA *look at each other.*)

ELECTRA: Is he well? Does he mention us?

IPHIGENIA: Does he mention me as a this or that?

CLYTEMNESTRA ONE (*turns, smiling*): There is some trouble, but he seems in good spirits, and he mentions you.

IPHIGENIA: Is there love in his mentioning? Oh, let me see.

CLYTEMNESTRA ONE: Your father has made plans. We are to pack and travel to Aulus.

IPHIGENIA: To visit? Me?

ELECTRA: And me, Mother?

CLYTEMNESTRA ONE: Only Iphigenia. To marry.

(IPHIGENIA *looks at* ELECTRA, *then* CLYTEMNESTRA ONE.)

IPHIGENIA: Oh, Mother, is it true? (*She runs to* CLYTEMNESTRA ONE, *taking the letter.*) It says I am to marry Achilles. But he is a God—a half-God, Achilles. Have you seen him? Is he as beautiful as they say?

CLYTEMNESTRA ONE: He is beautiful and strong—a great warrior and man.

IPHIGENIA (*runs to kneel and throws herself in her mother's lap*): You must help me, Mother, to get ready—to plan colors and clothing, and you must explain to me what I have done to make a man such as him, a God, love me, so that I may never stop doing it. (*She runs to embrace* ELECTRA.) I am to marry.

CLYTEMNESTRA ONE: Do you feel only eagerness to leave your poor mother alone?

IPHIGENIA: No, no. It is you he loves, Mother. You and Electra—you are in me and he loves you. We will make it so he never thinks to leave. I will plan menus and parties. How is it that I laugh and cry? Am I really to be given to a God?

(*And the tub, pushed by* AEGISTHUS, *comes rushing out from the dimness behind the net,* CLYTEMNESTRA TWO, *knife in hand, raging at the figure in the tub played by the actor who will be* ORESTES.)

CLYTEMNESTRA TWO: Like a fish he gapes and breathes. I will strike and suck from you the mystery of your life, Agamemnon.

AEGISTHUS: I've never done this before.

CLYTEMNESTRA TWO: There is a passion in our fingers, this handle, Aegisthus. (*And she is putting the knife into his hands.*) Our flesh; this steel. I saw a man once with a snake put into his hand. Up he came from sleep, this hissing creature in his grip.

He clutched it for fear that if he let it go, it would strike and kill him. And yet, could he hold it forever? What could he do?

AEGISTHUS: I hate snakes.

CLYTEMNESTRA TWO: I love you, I love you. (*She kisses him.*) Kill him.

(AEGISTHUS *backs up and she whirls away.*)

No, no, Clytemnestra is not coy, and that is her cunning. A blunt request is honest and fair; how else could it be made so openly? His lean muscled body shall be soft as a woman's.

(*She has moved back to* AEGISTHUS. *Together, gripping the knife, they have moved to stand over the tub. And there is thrashing from the tub, a muffled cry. She breaks away, yelling down into the tub.*)

No longer have your wishes any meaning. We are here now. Down ten years of roads and maps, ships and pathways, you have traveled to this tub. You have fled Aulus, triumphed at Troy, come back to me. I have seen too much of killing not to know the ways of doing it well. As you stuffed the mouth of my daughter using rags, I will stuff your mouth with blood. Aegisthus is my little husband now. Remember him? Uninterested in any war, he worries over papers and numbers. He tabulates and scribbles. (*And grabbing the end of the tub, she whirls it.*) He sits in candlelight. And where will you stab, Aegisthus? How many times?

AEGISTHUS: As many as you wish.

CLYTEMNESTRA TWO: Will you cut off a hand, let us say; or pluck out an eye?

AEGISTHUS: Of course.

CLYTEMNESTRA TWO: And will you make speeches, my love? Will you tell him of the honor, the glory for him to have his foot cut off because, as a result, the wind will rise, the fleet will sail, as if the wind could have an interest in feet burning or children . . . burning. (*Now she is bellowing to the figure in the tub.*) The wind has no feet, Agamemnon; it has no children. It does not know that they are valuable.

(*And the telephone begins to ring. In a kind of panic, all look about and upward. Like* AGAMEMNON, *they paw the air above them.*)

CLYTEMNESTRA ONE: Agamemnon!

IPHIGENIA: Father?

CLYTEMNESTRA ONE: I'm here.

AEGISTHUS: I'm here.

IPHIGENIA: Answer.

CLYTEMNESTRA TWO: ANSWER!

THE GIRL: Well, one of the more interesting facets of ourselves was our sneakies, these special uniforms which were all black so in the dark nobody could see us hardly at all. For lots of times we just wore 'em and went into people's houses for the fear of it, just to feel the fear of bein' in somebody's house—they didn't know you were there—they might come home any second—what would happen, oh, wow. So anyway, we had our sneakies on and the Angel says he wants Tex, who's from Texas, and us girls to be goin' out in this rich neighborhood and kill some gooks. I'm from Pennsylvania.

(*The ringing stops.* CLYTEMNESTRA ONE *stands looking toward* AGAMEMNON, *who is some distance from her, testing his knee. He pokes it, bends it. On the uppermost scaffolding,* IPHIGENIA *stands reading a letter.* AEGISTHUS *and* CLYTEMNESTRA TWO *are with the tub behind the hanging cargo net.* BECKY, JENNY, *and* SALLY *are scattered around the platforms.*)

IPHIGENIA: I think, Father, that I understand. Father?

(CLYTEMNESTRA ONE *steps toward* AGAMEMNON.)

CLYTEMNESTRA ONE: Hello.

AGAMEMNON: Clytemnestra, Clytemnestra, my knee is strange.

CLYTEMNESTRA ONE: What?

AGAMEMNON: Walking last night to speak to the sentries, my foot went between two rocks in the dark. I fell sideways.

CLYTEMNESTRA ONE: Let me see. (*Moving forward to examine the knee.*)

AGAMEMNON: Now it aches. Why should that be? My knee is a bendable thing. I had never wondered about it before. What is in a knee to make it work? It bends but one way.

CLYTEMNESTRA ONE: I don't know. How are you otherwise? I go through the encampment, but nowhere do I find signs of our daughter's wedding. When I ask about the preparations, I am met with glances that frighten me.

AGAMEMNON: Clytemnestra, I have thought to tell you this a hundred ways, but my lips and tongue can manage none of them. I have written what I cannot say. (*He hands her the letter and goes to lean against the scaffold while* CLYTEMNESTRA ONE *reads.*) I don't understand it. But they talk about me. They are here now. One of them—they're everywhere, listening, judging. They have dreamed of her—the Gods. It is their will, their desire. They brood in lust of our daughter. They talk of taking their love from me.

CLYTEMNESTRA ONE: Agamemnon, what is this?

AGAMEMNON (*gesturing to* PYLADES *who marches forward to hand a book, perhaps a copy of the* Iliad *to* CLYTEMNESTRA ONE): Helen, wife of my good brother Menelaus, has been kidnapped by conniving Trojans and their hearts must adorn my sword!

CLYTEMNESTRA ONE (*hurling the book away*): I know the troubles that brought you to this shore, but—

AGAMEMNON: I thought you would send her. (*He moves to touch her.*) I did not think you would be here to share this pain.

CLYTEMNESTRA ONE: What pain? You wrote me a letter promising a joyous day of marriage. I am here for her wedding.

AGAMEMNON (*seizes her shoulders*): I need only your faith in me.

CLYTEMNESTRA ONE: You say you did not know I would be here. But you summoned me.

AGAMEMNON (*still holding her*): I want your trust, Clytemnestra. I ask only for your trust.

CLYTEMNESTRA ONE: If this letter is true, there is no such thing as trust! There is no such word! (*She thrusts his hands aside.*) I am no fool, Agamemnon!

AGAMEMNON: You are unfair. You burden me with unjust blame. I am not blameless, but I am no monster. (*He is moving around her.*) What is it in you that you must call your husband monster? Yes, I am your husband, our daughter's father, but I am also a king and general. This kidnapping is more than the disappearance of one woman. We have been violated and threatened. This venture on the part of the barbarians is not accidental, but it is a probe to test our will. One man sent into our midst to steal one woman, and now they await our reaction, which must come. Our sudden towering sails shall turn their shoreline black with shadow; and they will sue for peace at the sight of us. They cannot truly wish to fight unless they find some pulse of weakness beating in us, some sweet softness corrosive in our blood. Then our danger will have begun. No woman nor anything in Greece will be safe, and it will not be just one man who disgraces and robs us, but bands of raiders, and then small fleets until one day an armada closes in upon the sea around us and we are lost. (*From a distance, he faces her.*) You do not believe this because it is of the kind of knowledge that men have that I am speaking. (*He is crossing to her.*) But there are nations in this world—these eyes have seen them—men who have no grace nor mercy—they plunder for no reason but their own hungers. From these inhuman creatures we must protect ourselves. And even if it were not so simple—if it were more complicated, which it could be—because there are times when the people who threaten you do it without validity—not without true grievance. But is that any reason to allow them to kill you? Because it is possible they have the right.

CLYTEMNESTRA ONE: Agamemnon, you must—

AGAMEMNON: Answer my question. Is there any reason to allow them to kill us?

CLYTEMNESTRA ONE: No. Of course not. But—

AGAMEMNON: Then go from this place.

CLYTEMNESTRA ONE: But these papers declare that my child must die!

AGAMEMNON: We are chained here. The most powerful army in the world, and Iphigenia is the key. In smoke and the moon, in the innards of a blessed and God-sent bird, Calchas has read that Iphigenia, though she be innocent, must die.

IPHIGENIA (*standing with her father's letter in her hand. Yet she speaks upward as if her father is somewhere high above her*): Father, I tremble when I think of it.

AGAMEMNON: The Goddess of this place demands a virgin's death.

IPHIGENIA: When in love he holds me, Father—Achilles, who is of the blood of a Goddess—when we are one in love, will I be also, as he, divine?

CLYTEMNESTRA TWO: AGAMEMNON!

(*The phone begins to ring.*)

CLYTEMNESTRA ONE (*to* AGAMEMNON): The wind has no children!
CLYTEMNESTRA TWO: The wind has no feet or children!
CLYTEMNESTRA ONE (*moving forward as* CLYTEMNESTRA TWO *is moving backward, ripping up Agamemnon's letter*): The wind has no children. It does not know that they are valuable.
CLYTEMNESTRA TWO: Who takes my time away from me?

(*As* CLYTEMNESTRA ONE *tosses the paper at* AGAMEMNON *and runs to embrace* CLYTEMNESTRA TWO.)

CLYTEMNESTRA ONE: Who takes my time away from me? Who takes my time?
THE SPEAKER: For not only are the systems of space large, but they are becoming continually larger. Every thirteen hundred million years, space doubles its linear dimensions, so that already there is eight times as much space as when the first radioactive rock solidified and there is perhaps more than one hundred times as much as when the earth itself was torn out of the sun. With every tick of the clock, the distance of the width of space increases by hundreds and hundreds of thousands of miles. With every tick of the clock. It is a black immensity in which we float like singular particles of dust . . . bits of air . . . molecules in peculiar exile.
AGAMEMNON (*kneeling, praying to the Godheads*): I say to you, Gods, if your word is cruel, is it any less your holy and blessed word. I don't know, but I think we have no right to resist when, if this price were being asked of some other, we would compel that payment. I believe we have no choice, though once I thought we did, and though it is the cruelty of our natures to make it seem we do—and so the pain in me—though it is Clytemnestra who makes all the noises of suffering—my pain is monstrous. Do you hear me? Do you hear me, Gods? This child's death torments me! Who hears me? (*He opens his eyes, looks about.*) Who hears me?
THE SPEAKER: I hear you, Agamemnon.
AGAMEMNON: Who hears me?
CLYTEMNESTRA TWO (*at the tub*): Our knife, Aegisthus, will sever

the threads that lock in his life. Since he wishes to speak of monstrous pain, we will teach it to him. Hold his arm to begin the lesson.

(AEGISTHUS *seizes the arm of the man in the tub.*)

To have your skin cut deep and quickly, Agamemnon . . . (*She lunges.*) . . . is that monstrous pain? Or to have straight, slow slices. Or is it simply to know the knife is near? Can you define it? In terms of your own flesh, I mean. (*She moves to the end of the tub.*) Do you know for instance that a man is all strings, all bits of hair, and an eye and knife deft and quick enough could sever him apart thread by string. Would that be monstrous?

(*The man in the tub groans.*)

You mutter, you murmur. What is monstrous pain?!

(*And she thrusts into the tub, her own voice a scream that is joined by the cry of the man in the tub, one loud wail that ends as a yelp from* AGAMEMNON, *sitting poking at his knee.*)

AGAMEMNON: I have indeed hurt my knee. I did not bend it out of the ordinary trying to kick a guard. A trivial thing—yet it hurts. I have done a drawing of it. (*As* THE SPEAKER *holds up a drawing of the knee.*) In order to try and see what might have happened inside it when I fell among the rocks the other night. It is so odd, bending so extremely in one way and so little in the others. Also it has made me curious about . . . the elbow . . . which bends only in the opposite direction. (*Now he demonstrates how the knee bends one way while the elbow bends the other. This stands him on one leg, his right leg and right elbow bending.*)

CLYTEMNESTRA ONE: I have been looking for you.

AGAMEMNON: Do you see the way I suspect they work? I'm curious to learn more of them.

CLYTEMNESTRA ONE: They have told Iphigenia. Her eyes, agleam as if with love, let loose tears. Where were you, Agamemnon? You must stop this thing.

AGAMEMNON: I can not.

CLYTEMNESTRA ONE: You do not even hesitate.

AGAMEMNON: Because the truth is not elusive, I do not hesitate. (*He is pacing away.*)

CLYTEMNESTRA ONE: What truth? Where is this truth, and where is Iphigenia in any of it? Like dogs you do the tricks of foolish Menelaus, who can not keep his wife—but between this departure of Helen and our daughter's death, nothing real exists—do you see—unless you put it there.

AGAMEMNON: I put nothing. No. It is Calchas.

(*Under the booth,* CLYTEMNESTRA TWO *leans against the net, watching.*)

CLYTEMNESTRA ONE: It happens within you. All within you—that is what I am saying.

AGAMEMNON: She will be given to a God.

CLYTEMNESTRA ONE: I will damn you to that same God, Agamemnon. (*Her hands are moving to his face.*) I swear it. His bones will hold you. He will kiss you at the rim of hell.

AGAMEMNON: Don't . . . touch me!

CLYTEMNESTRA TWO: Aegisthus, do you know me where I am an animal? (*Entwining herself on the ropes of the net.*)

AEGISTHUS (*moves behind her, hands around her waist*): I have loved you, yes, . . . touched you.

(AGAMEMNON *is trying to remove* CLYTEMNESTRA ONE's *hands from his face. But it is as if she is enormously strong.*)

CLYTEMNESTRA TWO: I am an animal.

AEGISTHUS: Flesh. So are we all.

CLYTEMNESTRA TWO: I am full within myself. I paint my body. (*She takes* AEGISTHUS' *hand to her breast.*) I decorate not my clothing, but my skin. I am water and oil, sea salt. I crawl up, thinking, from the sea.

IPHIGENIA: Father, where are you?

(*She runs to* AGAMEMNON, *who breaks free from* CLYTEMNESTRA ONE *and grabs* IPHIGENIA.)

I dreamed of you: monkeys carried snakes. They murdered you. There were many corridors of shelves of bottles and in one of them, in a greenish-yellow liquid, you were sealed. I beat upon the glass. They said I could not speak to you. You have been cut in battle, Father, what is the feeling?

AGAMEMNON: It is not the same. No, no.

IPHIGENIA: And will I be given wine? I must have wine.

AGAMEMNON: Of course.

IPHIGENIA: Good, good. And will it be far to walk? I fear the walking. I would like to know whose hands will hold the knife. Will it tear my clothing? Will my wrists be bound? Will I be naked? I don't want to be naked. If it could be arranged that I could be carried, I would feel much better. There is nothing I can think of to want but dignity—I have thought and thought and it is dignity that I want. Not clothes or perfume. Clean water. All seem foolish. I could sit correctly, Father, I am sure. Properly. Erect as a queen. Or resting softly, if I were carried there. All would cheer and think me beautiful.

(PYLADES, *wearing the half-mask, comes running in and* AGAMEMNON *leaps to his feet.*)

PYLADES: Sir!

AGAMEMNON: I must go.

PYLADES: Sir, there's trouble, the man—

AGAMEMNON: All right, all right!

PYLADES: It's urgent!

(*Yet* IPHIGENIA *grabs* AGAMEMNON *as he moves to go.*)

IPHIGENIA: No. Please. And I know you are busy, and you are all good fine men who will only do what is right, but when I've been cut, will I be dead? I know I will no longer live, but when the knife is in me and I am no longer as I am . . . now . . . will I be merely changed or will I be nothing? Emptiness . . . or as I thought I would be joined to Achilles? I have fear, Father. Fear that is not ceremony, not burial, but disappearance. I fear, Father, that I shall vanish.

CLYTEMNESTRA ONE: She loves you, Agamemnon.

AGAMEMNON: Is this your curse?

CLYTEMNESTRA ONE: She loves you more than I have ever loved you. And I do not say that to hurt or surprise you, but only to make you see the thing you say you must destroy.

AGAMEMNON: But what of the inevitable and terrible losses to come if she is spared?

CLYTEMNESTRA ONE: There is no reason for this war. Helen loved the foreigner. Your brother is a dull, cold man and Helen left him. Dare you not acknowledge that she could long for a man from another land?

AGAMEMNON (*whirls to face her*): I have reports—proofs of kidnapping.

CLYTEMNESTRA ONE: Lies.

AGAMEMNON: Eyewitnesses saw her bound and gagged. Sentries were bribed; others murdered.

CLYTEMNESTRA ONE: It is only your pride.

AGAMEMNON: I would kill my daughter for pride?

CLYTEMNESTRA ONE: You have forgotten her.

AGAMEMNON (*taking* IPHIGENIA's *shoulders, he looks at her*): She is my child, whom I love and whom I will love even more in death.

MAN IN TUB: Father.

IPHIGENIA: What about my clothing? Will I be naked?

(AGAMEMNON'S *hands are still on his daughter.*)

CLYTEMNESTRA ONE: Her bones shall hold you as no daughter should a father!

IPHIGENIA: And I would be carried.

CLYTEMNESTRA ONE: Gagged with rot, her mouth shall press around your tongue.

IPHIGENIA: Have you nothing to tell me?

CLYTEMNESTRA ONE: What clothing will she wear?

PYLADES: Sir, we must go!

CLYTEMNESTRA ONE: Will she be carried or dragged?

MAN IN TUB: Father!

CLYTEMNESTRA ONE: Answer!

CLYTEMNESTRA TWO: Answer!

AGAMEMNON: Ohhh, God Apollo. Help me! (*He runs from them all.*)

IPHIGENIA: I dare not walk!

MAN IN TUB (*screaming*): FATHER!

(As CLYTEMNESTRA ONE *and* IPHIGENIA *are embracing, leaving.*)

CLYTEMNESTRA TWO (*crouching with* AEGISTHUS *beside the man flailing in the tub*): He comes to life. Our netted, incredulous fish, in order that he might die. Ohhh, no. This knife is your knife, Agamemnon. Stabbing gently. Kindly. The death it gives is meaningful. What is there to fear in this good, kind knife of sacrifice?

AEGISTHUS: Oh, my God.

CLYTEMNESTRA TWO: It's true.

AEGISTHUS: No, no—I dreamed—I just remembered—I dreamed that you dreamed of giving birth to a snake. Green and cruel, it came out of you. It looked like him. (*Gesturing at the tub.*) It wanted to embrace us. You nurtured it. I said, "Kill it."

CLYTEMNESTRA TWO (*laughing, moving toward him*): I had no such dream.

AEGISTHUS: Green and cruel, it squirmed out of you, and you held it to your breast to suck. It was your child, you said. "Orestes," you said. I demanded that you kill it. (*He gestures at the tub.*)

CLYTEMNESTRA TWO: I had no such dream!

AEGISTHUS: No! I did. I did. I had it. (*As he starts to flee.*) It looked like him.

CLYTEMNESTRA TWO: Aegisthus! (*Moving after him.*)

THE SPEAKER (*alone on the empty stage*): The activity of the brain is mainly electrical. Yet surprisingly enough, a thin section of brain tissue under a microscope looks like garden weeds.

(*As* AGAMEMNON *enters and picks up a bottle of whiskey sitting on the scaffolding. He starts drinking.*)

An electrochemical change in a single neuron—and there are some thirteen trillion in the body—institutes a series of changes all along the nerves so that an electrical impulse flows along its fiber like a spark along a fuse toward an explosion. . . . At each instant of our lives, in all the different parts of our body, some millions of neurons are firing, all the impulses leaping to the brain.

AGAMEMNON: A . . . ga . . . num . . . non. Aga . . . min . . . nom. (*He moves a step forward, trying very hard to concentrate.*) Aga . . . num . . . num! Aga . . . num . . . num? Shit. I . . . have a name,

that when I get drunk, I can't say it. I didn't ask to have such a
name and be . . . me. Did anyone ever hear Agamum . . . nun
. . . drunk or sober, request that he be me? But I am. I'm going let
my daughter die. (*Reeling to his feet.*) I get drunk. I fall down. I
pour wine in my ear. I pour it in my hair. (*Having staggered center
stage, his back to the audience, he urinates.*) I piss on rocks, and still
she is going to die. (*A soldier races up to him, whispers in his ear and
flees.*) Soldiers run up to me and say this has occurred, or that. I
don't give a fuck. A man has fallen off his horse and landed on his
sword. Am I to explain that? Take the man off the sword and give
the horse to someone else. I don't know. And there are platoons of
men at one far part of this island dividing the terrain into sectors
and preparing to fight because one believes the other stole its
aluminum tent poles.

THE SPEAKER: There are no aluminum tent poles.

AGAMEMNON: They are fighting over them. Who am I talking to?
(*He looks about.*) Who hears me?

THE GIRL: I hear you.

THE SPEAKER: I hear you, Agamemnon. (*As he drinks.*)

AGAMEMNON: I am here! I AM HERE! I see the surf destroying
itself on the shore, and I think, "Be like that. Be like that."
(*Whirling away from them.*) Oh, my God, I will make myself hard
and let the world destroy itself against me. What is a daughter? If
I took off running with my wine—now—how far would I get? I
so love my power. Would I feel it in the dark behind me to draw
me back? People do as I say. "Come here," I say, and they do. "Go.
Stand. Sit." It's amazing. So amazing. (*He crosses back, sits down
on the floor, staring outward.*) As a child, my brother and I would
play games of our father and uncle. (*Pause. He sits, remembering.*)
Uncle Thyestes would seduce his sister-in-law, our mother. And
then Atreus, our father, would make a dinner of our cousins, the
sons of Thyestes, and feed them to him. He would eat and vomit
them up. We would laugh. (*He laughs aloud, the sound trailing off.*)
I wanted to be Atreus, but Menelaus managed always to be our
father and I was foolish Thyestes, forever foolish and vomiting.
But now I am . . . Aga . . . num . . . num.

PYLADES: Agamemnon. (*He enters without the half-mask and carrying
Agamemnon's armor.*)

AGAMEMNON: Yes. YES!

PYLADES: It's time to get started.

AGAMEMNON: What? I know, I know.

PYLADES (*beginning to put the armor on* AGAMEMNON): Soon they will come for you. The great events of morning will be a storm to hurl us from this place. The men are excited. They know we leave soon. They talk of learning more of the wild beasts and men that fill the unknown world.

AGAMEMNON: I have never been to Asia Minor, but the people I have seen from Troy made little impression on me, though they are cunning. In six weeks we'll tack their tails to the wall.

(*Behind them* CLYTEMNESTRA ONE *has come to stand, watching.*)

PYLADES: To get some Trojan whores, Agamemnon. To drink wine in another man's land. Think of it. To leave their wives and sisters fat with seed. How can he ever drive us out when the children of his women belong in blood to us and they are there amid his people like little spies with faces that show forever what we have done to him.

AGAMEMNON: Buckle it tighter. It is good to feel this old skin of leather. Soon we go beyond the rim of this familiar sea.

(PYLADES *stands, smiling broadly.*)

CLYTEMNESTRA ONE: Look at you!

(AGAMEMNON *whirls, startled.*)

My God, I think we learn of one another, and I am not a fool to care for you. When I awoke to find you gone from our bed, I imagined you alone and heartsick somewhere in the night. I set out to console you, but—

AGAMEMNON: I need no consolation!

CLYTEMNESTRA ONE: I find you preening with this jackass, your brain lost in the glories of ruin and blood.

AGAMEMNON: Why do you never speak of survival? (*To* PYLADES:) Why does she never mention honor? (*And back to her:*) Why does this army mean nothing to you, these tens of thousands who languish here day after day eating half-rotten food so they may go finally into battle where they must risk their pride, their youth, their lives? Should only Clytemnestra risk nothing?

CLYTEMNESTRA ONE: I am losing my child.

AGAMEMNON: And so you must go on with dignity as I will in her honor.

CLYTEMNESTRA ONE: You cannot make me do this again! It cannot happen!

AGAMEMNON: We have other children. Last night, I put another into you—we drew him to this world. In my sleep, I saw him—a son. We must call him Orestes. Devote yourself to Electra.

CLYTEMNESTRA ONE: I have seen your unhappy face when for some small mischief you had to punish Iphigenia, simply scold her, and now you will kill her with pride. What am I to do?

AGAMEMNON: Go home, Clytemnestra! A ship can be readied within the hour to—

CLYTEMNESTRA ONE: But I am haunted! Already, I am—

AGAMEMNON: —Spare yourself this—

CLYTEMNESTRA ONE: You have killed my infant boy and now you will kill my girl. There are times already, Agamemnon, when that dead child torments me that I sleep in the arms of his killer.

AGAMEMNON: I have no fear of such a mewing little ghost.

CLYTEMNESTRA ONE: But what shall I do when both my children who are dead come back to sit on either side of our bed and you sleep and I sit, seeing the wishes of their eyes?

AGAMEMNON: I took you from a land of poverty and barbarism. Our land is a land of wealth. The Gods blessed and chose us. Your husband paid no tribute. He was a little man who fell sideways before my sword had even touched him and he knelt there panting until I clubbed him as I would a dog. I have no fear for his son who isn't even here.

CLYTEMNESTRA ONE: Again and again, I forget what you are!

AGAMEMNON: Then look at me! See me!

CLYTEMNESTRA ONE: Just as you have forgotten what you did.

AGAMEMNON (*whirling to stride away*): I haven't time for this.

CLYTEMNESTRA ONE: Even now I think of killing you, Agamemnon! My dead and squalling children demand it! (*Her words have stopped him.*) Like the knife they urge me to use, they shred all other hopes.

AGAMEMNON: I have not forgotten what I did, what we—

CLYTEMNESTRA ONE: But you have! And so you think that I have, too. I was a girl, though already a queen and a wife and mother. And one morning my husband runs to tell me barbarians have crossed our sacred borders. He is the king, but barely more than a boy. His cheeks are flushed, his eyes hot with fear. And by dusk you are there before me, his poor corpse strung through the heels on strips of leather, whose ends wrap round your fist. I watched you, my baby, mewing and sightless as a puppy in my arms, as you strode across that courtyard toward me.

AGAMEMNON: Women in captured towns huddle in shadows, Clytemnestra. They hold their children to them, they stare at the ground. You knelt in sunlight in the middle of that courtyard, your eyes—

CLYTEMNESTRA ONE: I know where I was. I know what I did. I told myself if I didn't move, you would not see me and I was trembling. I thought that if I did not look at you, you would pass me by and I could not take my eyes off you. I handed my son up to you to show our helplessness, to beg for mercy, his small mouth open to cry. You stood over me, like a beast dreaming that his prey adores him, my two men dangling from your hands. And then the child cried out, moving through the air, and I saw that you would kill him.

AGAMEMNON: I simply tossed him aside. I did not know his head would crack open on that wall. Seeing the look in your eye, I simply threw him in a kind of joy at what you would give me.

CLYTEMNESTRA ONE: But I reached to stop you—how could you not see that I reached to stop you?

AGAMEMNON: No. No.

(*As he reaches toward her and she knocks his hands away.*)

CLYTEMNESTRA ONE: It was impossible. I could not hold him. And then his little body was gone, and I held only your empty hands. Far behind me, there was a sound like teeth biting into an apple.

AGAMEMNON: You reached to bring me to you, as you draw me even now with your eyes and breath. You wanted me. (*He has her now.*)

CLYTEMNESTRA ONE: No.

AGAMEMNON (*as they struggle*): And now you lie, seeking to order the past by deceiving the present. (*Forcing her to the ground.*) You gave your permission.

CLYTEMNESTRA ONE: No!

AGAMEMNON: It was your wish in your eye.

CLYTEMNESTRA ONE: Kill no more that I love! Your name will come to mean no more than blood to me. I beg you!

AGAMEMNON: You held that child up like a gift.

CLYTEMNESTRA ONE (*flailing wildly against him*): Could I have wanted you pumping your filth into me with my dead husband and child beside me in the dirt? Is that what you think? It isn't possible! Agamemnon!

AGAMEMNON: What are we talking about? (*Breaking free of the embrace, struggling to stand.*)

CLYTEMNESTRA ONE: It is not possible!

AGAMEMNON: I don't know what we're talking about. Because none of this matters. None of it is of any consequence at all.

CLYTEMNESTRA ONE: But it is all that matters. It's everything. Think. Please find a way to lift us from this fate. I beg you, Agamemnon, think! Think!

(*His hands are clutching his head and* THE SPEAKER *eases up beside him, pointer in hand.*)

THE SPEAKER: Recent scientific brain experimentation has led— among other things—to the fact that the left lobe of the brain is verbal while the right lobe is mute, along with the knowledge that even when the left doesn't know what the right is doing, it persists in explaining the activities in which it finds itself involved. The more an anatomist, scalpel in hand, explores, the more he destroys that which he seeks to understand. Unlike the human heart which betrays its action by beating, the brain, laboring to solve the most complex of problems, is totally, utterly silent.

AGAMEMNON: But there is no wind, Clytemnestra. What am I to do when there is no wind and there must be? It is a common thing, yet it is not here. Where is it when it is not here? (*He looks about at the air.*)

THE SPEAKER (*whispering*): He's thinking.

AGAMEMNON: It is impossible. And I am a king and a general, and what if not to confront and make common the impossible is the purpose of a man who bears those names?

CLYTEMNESTRA ONE: It is not your motive.

AGAMEMNON: I swear it.

CLYTEMNESTRA ONE (*as he comes moving toward her*): Pride is your motive—vanity and power. The wind is your alibi and excuse.

AGAMEMNON: NOOOOO! (*And he pivots from her, ferocious in his denial.*)

THE SPEAKER (*pointing her pointer at his head*): An electrochemical change in a single neuron—say, here—(*and the pointer skips to his hand*) institutes a series of changes so that an electrical impulse flows along its fiber (*the pointer darts back to his head*) like a spark toward an explosion.

(AGAMEMNON *wheels about to face* CLYTEMNESTRA ONE.)

AGAMEMNON: You don't see the difficulty of every move, every decision, and all the while the petty considerations of the age rave at my heels like poor dumb dogs.

THE SPEAKER: It is the task of the brain . . . (*she points to his head*) to sort these billions of impulses, to establish priorities amid this popping.

AGAMEMNON: Always there are a thousand alternatives to every decision—each an unknown road whose end I ache to glimpse before I take our land forward upon it, so that I may know with certainty that it is the way most right for us. A thing I can not ever know. (*As he moves,* THE SPEAKER *follows, pointing to his head.*)

THE SPEAKER: It is the task of the brain to pronounce decisions amid these explosions. To deliver insights within this crackling, hissing skull.

AGAMEMNON: And this happens endlessly! Because there are moments whose dimensions demand the eye of a God to comprehend them when there are only men alive within them. And so I make decisions that in a God would be humane, but because I am a man, they are unnatural.

THE FIGURE (*appearing in the mask, the netted toga, beads, and bones of Calchas*): They are not unnatural. You do not speak of

118DAVID RABE

the reasons. You do not speak of the issues. I am Calchas, the prophet. I will tell the reasons.

AGAMEMNON: Priest, she torments me.

THE FIGURE: I will bring peace and harmony. (*He moves forward, carrying a briefcase.*)

CLYTEMNESTRA ONE: Calchas, I honor you; I know your name.

THE FIGURE: Little else but my name. Not of the secrets these fingers spread now before your eyes can read. There are things to be seen by touching. (*He places his briefcase on the ground.*)

AGAMEMNON: Forgive me, Priest, if I offended you. For a moment, I could see nothing but the wish of my child to live.

THE FIGURE: It is only love of one another that confuses you.

CLYTEMNESTRA ONE: Priest, I beg you—let me understand.

THE FIGURE (*gently*): You seek to change him, Clytemnestra, and because he cares for you, he feels weakness. I am not a cold man. I understand. Believe that I understand. And believe that I feel, after your large grief, something that is mine alone. I am mystery to you, a voice come to tell you that your daughter must die. You would demand, "By what right? What authority?" And because I respect you, because I want no human pain to exist if there is a way it can be avoided, I will refuse the temptation to feel dishonored by your request, which I know, if it is made at all, must be made in doubt of my word and power. I will explain. We are creatures of reason. I will make of this meeting a moment in which words and goodwill shared among men make mystery less mystery. There is peace to be given by reason. Please, Agamemnon, kneel also.

AGAMEMNON: Yes. (*He kneels while* THE FIGURE *opens his briefcase and takes out a small object wrapped in cloth.*)

THE FIGURE: Clytemnestra, listen. (*Beginning to spread on the cloth the many small hunks of bone wrapped in the cloth.*)

CLYTEMNESTRA ONE: Priest, know that I wish to hear you. I ache for the rest you offer.

THE FIGURE: Then listen. There are lines of blood on the small bones of a bird, and they have meaning. A triangular bit of stone can alter the importance of a winglike pattern of sinew. My fingers read these signs, these many intricate signs. The bird is brushed against me and then put into flight. He soars to touch against the cloud citadels of heaven to eavesdrop upon the whispering Gods within. Returned, slit open, his warm birdheart beats between these fingers I now thrust toward you, and they learn of his journey. There are colors and hidden sounds, deep pockets of mucus that, looked into, have voice. Purple is a cry for help. Scarlet mucus means innocence. Amber is royalty. (*He rises.*) Three successive days I read it, Clytemnestra: our ships frozen on a summer sea, and nothing possible to free them but the blood of a girl. Blood, do you see? To melt all ice and unleash our imprisoned ships. Because of our outrageous numbers in this harbor, the Goddess of this place has grown offended, and so she has hidden the wind. Consequently, it is her wish—the wish of Artemis—that before we can depart, a recompense be paid, a recompense of blood, the blood of royalty and innocence, the royal and innocent blood of Iphigenia.

AGAMEMNON (*kneeling and bowed over*): Did you see? It is as I told you: she is and has been the price from the beginning. (*He straightens.*) Our ships do not shiver with the smallest breeze. All rot in the degradation of lacking a thing so common as wind, a thing so common as children. (*He rises to his feet.*) I do not fear the truth. She is a child and the world teems with them. All put here for the use of the Gods, and now Calchas in wisdom and goodness has told us that use.

CLYTEMNESTRA ONE: Priest, could you say it again?

AGAMEMNON: She belongs to the Gods.

THE FIGURE: The Gods shall have her.

CLYTEMNESTRA ONE: I feel the rocks shall drink her blood.

AGAMEMNON: Woman, be careful that you—

CLYTEMNESTRA ONE: I feel dirt will have her.

THE FIGURE: Do not refuse the peace I offer.

CLYTEMNESTRA ONE: Her dried blood will look like moss upon the stones.

THE FIGURE (*His hand on Clytemnestra One's head*): I am the final authority, offering peace and rest. The tongue with which I speak is rooted in the mouth of God. I am His lips and tongue.

CLYTEMNESTRA ONE: You are His vomit!

AGAMEMNON (*slapping her*): He is the power that guides us through the world!

CLYTEMNESTRA ONE (*rising up and backing away*): No, I deny!

THE FIGURE: It does no good to deny. You will have no rest till you accept my words.

CLYTEMNESTRA ONE (*covering her face*): I deny.

THE FIGURE (*outraged*): You must accept my words! Only then will her name and yours, also, and mine and Agamemnon's be sung with reverence into time, for to make possible the sailing of these ships will be to make possible the beginning of a miracle!

AGAMEMNON: Priest, humble yourself no further. She blames us because the Gods kill her children.

CLYTEMNESTRA ONE: The entrails of a bird are garbage.

THE FIGURE: Only when we see beyond ourselves do we truly begin to see. We must see the concerns of others. (*He crosses away, taking the briefcase and bones with him.*)

AGAMEMNON: You are consumed with yourself. (*He follows* THE FIGURE *away, leaving her.*)

CLYTEMNESTRA ONE: No, it is you. All of you. In postures of mourning, you will gather together, and you will look at the sky as if the sky could be pertinent while she dies at your feet, a gagging, butchered girl.

(*As* SALLY, BECKY, PYLADES, *and* JENNY *enter. They lower the cargo net and spread it on the floor.*)

All because you are kings and generals and priests to whom even the wind you believe must bow if only you can find the means to tempt it. Why can you not understand that a thing in this universe can be deaf to you? Not unconcerned, or opposed, but deaf beyond response.

(THE FIGURE *as Calchas returns carrying a bowl of blood, as he moves to stand on the net spread on the floor.*)

You trade my daughter for your delusions!

IPHIGENIA: Priest, I honor you. I honor you.

(*Moving to stand before* THE FIGURE, *she kneels, he kneels facing her, suddenly tearing open the front of her dress. He begins to paint her body and murmur.*)

THE SPEAKER: Even the briefest consideration of uncivilized people everywhere and in all ages shows that terror lurked down the primeval street, in the primeval forest, over the primeval sea, terror and magic, and the most common defense of all—the human sacrifice—some awesome ritual by which bodies are piled up to the invisible and monuments are built to the bodies.

IPHIGENIA: Father, he paints me. Calchas paints me. The ropes are tight.

AGAMEMNON (*rushing forward to her*): Child, I have outrage at what has been done to us, at time and this life and how they have conspired to make it impossible for us to know one another as we should, through all the changes of many years.

CLYTEMNESTRA ONE: Give him nothing for his lies! (*Bending to* IPHIGENIA *from the opposite side.*)

AGAMEMNON: Take her! Guards!

CLYTEMNESTRA ONE (*as* PYLADES *in a mask rushes forward to grab her and drag her back*): No! Don't listen!

AGAMEMNON: Iphigenia, forgive me.

(THE FIGURE *pushes* IPHIGENIA *backward to lie on the net. He rises, the bowl of blood in hand.*)

CLYTEMNESTRA ONE: See how he lies to make you think of your death as more his suffering than your own! You are to return to him his innocence because he suffers for his crime even as he does it. And yet he does it.

AGAMEMNON (*rushing to* CLYTEMNESTRA ONE): You are a pit, Clytemnestra!

CLYTEMNESTRA ONE: He lies to make your death seem a gift you give rather than a deceit and robbery done to you!

(*As the net with* IPHIGENIA *lying in it begins to rise, Calchas with her.*)

IPHIGENIA: I will give you children, Father; grandsons!

CLYTEMNESTRA ONE: Look into hatred of him, Iphigenia!

AGAMEMNON: You are a pit. You think forever in terms of that cell inside you. You would hold the world there and lock it in that darkness! (*Whirling, he runs back to kneel beneath the risen net.*) Iphigenia, look to the Goddess! The Goddess will guide you!

IPHIGENIA (*singing*):

> Will I circle in the air?
> Will I tremble as a smaller start?
> Birds pass by like boats in the water.
> I am the sound of snow afar.
> I fall and wonder
> How I am more, more than I, can explain
> Am I the perfect smallness of the rain?

(*High above them,* THE FIGURE *kneels astride* IPHIGENIA, *the knife and beaker of blood in his hands above her.*)

CLYTEMNESTRA ONE (*as* PYLADES *releases her, now that the net has risen*): Why is it that the Gods have always the minds of old men hungry for the bodies of young girls? Why is that, Agamemnon? I swear it to you—had I known the prize her purity was to win for her, I would have coupled her with a dog—the first passing cur.

AGAMEMNON: I am your king and husband, Clytemnestra; know that and be still.

CLYTEMNESTRA ONE: But I say you are murdering our daughter.

AGAMEMNON: I am twice your ruler!

CLYTEMNESTRA ONE: And if you slaughter a child—

AGAMEMNON: I do not murder—

CLYTEMNESTRA ONE: —you are no king or husband.

(*As* AEGISTHUS *comes rushing forward with the tub while* CLYTEMNESTRA TWO *comes storming toward the tub, dagger poised.*)

AGAMEMNON: I do not slaughter! I sacrifice! I sacrifice! (*He is fleeing.*)

CLYTEMNESTRA TWO: I SACRIFICE!

(*And* CLYTEMNESTRA TWO *plunges her knife into the tub, and* IPHIGENIA *screams as the figure in the tub writhes.*)

CLYTEMNESTRA ONE: I SACRIFICE!

CLYTEMNESTRA TWO: You have murdered children that I loved . . .

CLYTEMNESTRA ONE: You have murdered children that I loved . . .

CLYTEMNESTRA TWO: You have murdered love in me.

CLYTEMNESTRA ONE: You have murdered love in me.

CLYTEMNESTRA TWO: You have hurt and left me lonely, but for none of these reasons . . .

CLYTEMNESTRA ONE: For none of these reasons . . .

CLYTEMNESTRA TWO: For no reason you can ever name or know, I am going to cut your life out of you. There is a tree, Agamemnon, that I wish to see grow. I am told your blood will give it life. And so, because I wish this tree to grow, and because it is my whim and appetite at this moment to see you die, I make this thrust into your flesh.

(*As she thrusts fiercely into the tub,* AEGISTHUS *is backing away.*)

Do you know, if I were to think of this as cruelty, I could not do it. But it is not, and there is dignity in it. And so, because to kill you is a pointless thing, and a pointless thing is what I wish to do, I will make this final thrust . . . (*the knife is rising*) . . . into your flesh and you . . . in some few seconds will be also a bride of Achilles. He will kiss you at the rim of hell! (*She stabs.*)

IPHIGENIA (*in the net above the tub as* THE FIGURE *leaves her*): They stood in rows along the pathway, eating bread and cheese, drinking wine. One tried to lie beside me. Guards pushed him off. I did not understand. And then I did and I felt separate from everything. They were an army gathered to await their war. I was a young girl put out before them. They had thronged there piled among the rocks and I heard the roaring vulgar sound they made until I heard nothing.

CLYTEMNESTRA TWO (*staring into the tub*): Look at him.

AEGISTHUS (*cannot bear the sight*): My God.

CLYTEMNESTRA TWO: Look at him.

AEGISTHUS (*reels backward*): They are screaming in the streets.

CLYTEMNESTRA TWO: Do you know, Aegisthus, I have let the life run out of a king? A king's dying is larger than a daughter's. It is impossible—impossible that I could marry a man who would kill our children. I could not kill my husband. I am not such a woman.

THE FIGURE: It is time for Orestes. Time that Orestes come.

(*High in the scaffolding, he wears his Levi's jacket, boots, trousers.*)

CLYTEMNESTRA TWO: Apollo!

THE FIGURE (*coming down*): It is time that Orestes arrive with his story . . . understanding nothing.

AEGISTHUS (*backing away*): Understanding nothing?

THE FIGURE: With his story and hatred and knife. And it will not be his story that will matter, nor will it be his hatred, but only the knife.

CLYTEMNESTRA TWO: Aegisthus . . . ! (*She looks toward him.*)

THE FIGURE (*moving to the side of the tub, looking down into it*): When you have it, you live.

CLYTEMNESTRA TWO: Aegisthus! The knife! What is he saying?

THE FIGURE: You live until you lose it.

CLYTEMNESTRA TWO: I struck. Where is it?

(*She is seeking the knife in the tub, plunging her arms in again and again, and though she grows bloody, she cannot find the knife, not even the body.*)

The knife, the knife! It entered into him. You are not fair, Apollo.

THE FIGURE: I know.

CLYTEMNESTRA TWO: Vanished into him. . . .

THE FIGURE: Through the flesh of the father . . .

CLYTEMNESTRA TWO: Fell through him. I could not hold it.

CLYTEMNESTRA ONE (*off to the side, staring at* CLYTEMNESTRA TWO *struggling in the tub*): It sank as if he were enormous.

CLYTEMNESTRA TWO: Falling past my groping hands a hundred times.

THE FIGURE: To the hand of the son.

CLYTEMNESTRA TWO: Apollo, no!

THE FIGURE: If I am Apollo, should I not then hate the dark and the dark conjuring incantations of the Pythian Princess whom I adore? I feel I am Dionysus, Apollon of the pit, prince of light and bearer of darkness. I feel I should lift men, though they call me Apollo. I love the pitiful small reeds of their bones. I wish the earth to spin faster, and men to learn of the universe until they uncover their natures and drown in madness. I must have Orestes. I embrace you. I must have Orestes! (*Touching her face with his fingertips.*) I embrace you in my embrace of dear love, Clytemnestra. (*He is so gentle with her.*) And the weaker you grow, the tinier your cries, the greater my loss of you. Where is Orestes?

CLYTEMNESTRA TWO (*sinking to her knees*): Apollo! I did not mean to lose it!

THE FIGURE: I KNOW. WHERE IS ORESTES? I MUST HAVE HIM!

CLYTEMNESTRA ONE (*from off to the side*): He shall not be born!

CLYTEMNESTRA TWO: Oh, my God!

THE FIGURE: Oh, yes. There. (*He looks at* CLYTEMNESTRA ONE.) He is there. My Orestes. (*He moves to* CLYTEMNESTRA ONE, *as* CLYTEMNESTRA TWO *collapses.*) I had forgotten, but he is . . . (*kneeling in worship before* CLYTEMNESTRA ONE, *his hands on her belly*) . . . here. Put here by good Agamemnon. And he will arrive, my Orestes, to see me and use me to rid the world of all Clytemnestras. What friends we will be! Apollo and Orestes. (*His hands are caressing her belly.*)

CLYTEMNESTRA ONE (*she pushes at the hands, trying feebly to remove them*): No. I say, no. (*Yet she cannot resist them. Her struggle ceases.*)

THE FIGURE (*holds her as* THE SPEAKER *is approaching*): Yet we shall. Yet we shall. Oh, belly, we await you. I embrace you. Oh, belly. Oh, beautiful, beautiful belly.

ALL (*singing from wherever they are, a minor key*):

Bubbles mark the ocean for a moment where we drown.
Bubbles mark the ocean for a moment where we drown.

THE SPEAKER (*touching Clystemnestra One's belly with the pointer*): In a place like this, we all begin. Deep within the body of another.

(*As the lights fade to black.*)

ACT TWO

On the scaffolding, a statue of AEGISTHUS *lies on its side. The tub is midstage left with* CLYTEMNESTRA TWO *near it. Downstage left,* THE FIGURE *kneels before* CLYTEMNESTRA ONE, *his hands on her belly, as she is sinking down onto the floor.* BECKY, SALLY, JENNY, *and* PYLADES *are scattered about the stage.* THE SPEAKER *steps forward.*

THE SPEAKER: As we travel along now, moving here and there in space and time and time and space, shall we see our earth come into being as a burning ball of gas which gradually cools? In due time, shall we see life appear?

(*Now both* CLYTEMNESTRA *One and* CLYTEMNESTRA TWO *begin to move and pant with the throes of giving birth,* THE FIGURE *tending* CLYTEMNESTRA ONE.)

Grass and weeds, fish and frogs, apes and mice and trees appear. Lizards, dogs, ticks, flowers, acorns, horses, spiders, whales, orchids, robins, leeches, snails, daisies, fox, cats, stallions, stickbugs, cardinals, crows, pythons and monarch butterflies. And finally, shall there be among them, man!

(ORESTES *peeps out from the tub, as both* CLYTEMNESTRAS *scream and collapse. Startled, he ducks back down into the tub.* THE FIGURE *pulls the knife from between the legs of* CLYTEMNESTRA ONE. *Leaving the knife on the floor,* THE FIGURE *backs away.*)

Shall he arrive at last to take possession of his tiny buzzing bee in space . . . the hissing, humming thing on which he finds himself adrift and starboard of the moon.

(ORESTES *slowly reappears, wary and wrapped in the placentalike gory net in which his father died.*)

126

Is it with astonishment and terror that he views the cold stellar reaches of his future, the earth, and himself?

(*As* ORESTES *steps out of the tub.*)

Is it with rage and venom that he steps into his world? Is it with love or dread that he arrives?

(ORESTES *is staring at the knife lying on the floor. He is wrapped in gore, covered in blood. Both* CLYTEMNESTRA *stare at him.*)

CLYTEMNESTRA ONE (*backing toward* CLYTEMNESTRA TWO): What . . . do you want?

CLYTEMNESTRA TWO: What?

ORESTES (*to* CLYTEMNESTRA ONE *and* TWO *who are together, as he moves toward them*): Life. To breathe. To breathe.

CLYTEMNESTRA ONE: Who are you?

ORESTES (*to* CLYTEMNESTRA ONE *and* TWO): I don't know. For sure. I think I know.

CLYTEMNESTRA TWO: Who?

THE FIGURE (*from under the scaffold*): Orestes!

(*Both* CLYTEMNESTRAS *are retreating as* ORESTES, *moving after them, has come upon the knife.*)

CLYTEMNESTRA ONE: No.

CLYTEMNESTRA TWO: No.

ORESTES: (*following* CLYTEMNESTRA ONE *and* TWO, *he gestures with the knife as he would with a stick as he speaks*): I have been in exile.

(*They scream and run from the stage, leaving* ORESTES *staring in bafflement.* THE FIGURE, *dressed in Levi's, a Levi's jacket, and boots is approaching. His hair is still up, or in a ponytail.*)

THE FIGURE: I know who you are.

ORESTES: Hello.

(BECKY, *in Levi's and a blouse tied at her belly, enters with a towel to clean the blood of birth from* ORESTES.)

THE FIGURE: Hello. Don't be worried or afraid. You are Orestes.

ORESTES: Oh, I know. Of course.

THE FIGURE: It's good to be Orestes.

ORESTES: I feel . . . it is good. I feel it is great. Am I not great? I am here now. At last my exile is over.

THE FIGURE: Son of Agamemnon, Atreus, Tantalus.

(ORESTES *faces* THE FIGURE.)

You move away from them, up from them. You progress.

ORESTES (*to* BECKY): I have never been here before.

THE FIGURE: But you are now. Are you hungry?

ORESTES: What?

THE FIGURE: What do you know of your mother and father?

ORESTES: Who are you? May I ask?

THE FIGURE (*approaching* ORESTES, *in a conspiratorial manner*): I feel I must speak to you of your mother—I must speak to you of your father—yet it is complex—who am I to tell you? Your father is dead, Orestes.

ORESTES: Dead? But I must see him.

THE FIGURE: Your mother did something terrible to your father.

ORESTES: What? What did she do? What did my good mother do to my good father?

THE FIGURE: (*unveiling a kind of bust of* AGAMEMNON; *it is a fragment of what was once a larger statue*): There's nothing left of him but this!

ORESTES: This is not my father. No, no—not this cold stone. (*Taking the stone into his hands.*)

THE FIGURE: It is his likeness—a shell, nothing more. But even in this fragment, do you not see the inherent honor of his gaze, the nobility of those matchless eyes. Once this statue stood atop his grave and was a shrine that aroused in many a huge devotion. He seemed to gesture toward the horizon that had once held the limitless vista of his ideals.

ORESTES: Shall I put a lock of hair upon his grave? Where is it? I want to pray for him.

THE FIGURE (*indicating the tub*): Over there.

ORESTES (*moves to the tub*): I will.

THE FIGURE: Beware of Tantalus, however. Or have you no concern for him?

ORESTES: Who?

THE FIGURE: Tantalus—your great-great-grandfather. Do you wish to put a lock of hair upon his ancient dirt, also? Even though he suffers at this very moment deep at the center of the earth in Hell.

ORESTES: I have a relative in Hell?

(*He looks down into the tub.*)

THE FIGURE: Do you not feel his eyes looking up through all the layers of the earth to you? Peer down the hole.

ORESTES: I have no wish to acknowledge a relative in Hell.

(*Trying to back away.*)

THE FIGURE: Peer down the hole.

(*Forcing him to look into the tub.*)

ORESTES: This . . . you said . . . was my father's grave.

THE FIGURE: It is all one.

ORESTES: I think not. (*Pulling free, backing away.*) And there is a chill. Something icy rising from it.

THE FIGURE: Are you cold—you look uncomfortable.

ORESTES: A little. (*As* BECKY *enters with clothing for* ORESTES. *She helps him dress.*)

THE FIGURE: Here's some clothing, trousers and a shirt with the face of Tantalus upon the front. Wear it with pride.

(*Quickly,* ORESTES *examines the face upon his shirt.*)

ORESTES: Tantalus? But his eyes are kind. How can he be in Hell if his eyes are so kind?

THE FIGURE: Wear it to show you have no shame—to show you understand that shame is a negative, pointless thing. He is your ancestor, your roots.

(BECKY *is helping* ORESTES *dress at tub's edge.*)

I feel him looking up, don't you? His grief and confusion arise like starving dogs. How is it possible, he wonders, that his descendant has grown to such perfection as you? Poor Tantalus. He cooked and fed his son to the Gods, yearning blindly to trick their divine bellies into filling with the flesh and blood of Tantalus. He loved his son. He loved himself.

ORESTES (*disgusted*): That's a terrible thing.

THE FIGURE: It was a darkness that moved in him.

ORESTES: It no longer moves in me.

THE FIGURE: Of course not.

ORESTES: I don't understand it.

THE FIGURE: He is the oldest of your house, however, so he is often discussed. You should know of him. There are those who say he leapt full grown from the lip of God. Others say he lived as a half-beast for many, many years, and then, touched by a God, he became man.

ORESTES: I suspect not.

THE FIGURE: Oh?

ORESTES: It is just my feeling, but I would guess he only looked like a man, seemed one—and was more the beast until a longer time went by, and many others were born, each becoming more and more nearly as I am.

(*Music begins softly, an introduction.*)

THE FIGURE: The culmination.

ORESTES: I feel I am.

BECKY (*to* ORESTES): Sing to me, won't you sing to me?

SALLY: Do you sing?

THE FIGURE: Oh, yes; do sing. Sing.

(*He backs away as* ORESTES *quickly kisses* SALLY, *and begins to sing.*)

ORESTES:

> I wake up in the morning
> The morning's aflame
> Lines of wonder mark my brain.

(*And as* ORESTES *sings, his audience,* THE FAMILY, *waves lighted Zippo lighters back and forth, as they listen and back farther and farther away.*)

> In the morning sun awakening
> I wear a lion's mane,
> In some magic corner of my brain.

I feel taller than before
And in the mellow air
I hear how I am so much more.
Oooorestes. Oooorestes
Great, great, great Orestes.
Great, great, great Orestes.

(*Singing, his eyes closed, he is now alone except for* THE GIRL *leaning against an upstage bit of scaffolding.*)

THE GIRL: We didn't know how many people or what kind of weapons, and we went around looking to see how many people while meanwhile Tex, Sally, and Sissie were tying people up— and Becky, oh, wow, was yelling terrible because the girl she was fighting was so strong and biting her and Tex came running in to stab the girl in the stomach, I guess, because I saw her grab down there.

ORESTES (*startled by this stranger*): Are you . . . talking to me? (*He crosses toward her.*)

THE GIRL: Hi.

ORESTES: Did you hear my song and came to speak to me? And those terrible things you were talking about—were they what was done to my good father?

(*But she turns, leaving him.*)

Wait!

(*He is puzzled, looking after her, as behind him* BECKY, SALLY, *and* JENNY *rush on carrying books and papers, a book bag.*)

BECKY: Orestes, hello.

(*They all say "Hello, hello," as* THE SPEAKER, *smiling, enters. The girls all wear Levi's and blouses, yet they have on their half-masks.*)

ORESTES: You know my name. (*He recognizes* BECKY *and moves toward her.*) You heard my song. I saw you before.

SALLY (*stopping him*): Apollo sent us to help you.

JENNY: Abbadon.

BECKY: We have been sent by your friend, God of Reason and the pit.

JENNY (*handing him books, papers, pencils*): To help you learn. We're
here to help you learn.

BECKY (*opening a book*): It is written in the journal of Aegisthus that
you are dead. "The infant of Orestes was killed by me," he has
written.

(*Referring to her book.*)

ORESTES: But I am here.

SALLY (*coming to his side*): Yet other things are written. And you are
here.

BECKY: Of course he is.

JENNY: He's here.

ORESTES: I'm here.

SALLY: It is written that you're here because at the time your father
returned from Troy, your mother saved you from murderous
Aegisthus.

(*She is referring to another book.*)

BECKY: On page ninety-nine she sent you off to Phocis to live with
your grandparents. See. (*She points.*)

SALLY: But there are difficulties, contradictions.

JENNY: Yes, yes, because it is also written on one hundred twelve
that on the day of your father's murder, it was not your mother
who saved you but a certain good and gracious nurse named
Arsinoe that let you live.

BECKY: Do you want to take some notes? You ought to take some
notes.

JENNY AND SALLY AND BECKY (*shouting*): Take some notes!

SALLY: It is written that the nurse was named Laodomaia!

BECKY: Gellissa is also written!

JENNY: Aegisthus killed somebody.

ORESTES: How is Laodomaia spelled?

BECKY (*as* SALLY *starts spelling names*): Arsinoe is very probable.

ORESTES: Laodomaia, Arsinoe, Gell—

SALLY: Clytemnestra could have done it!

BECKY: Someone put an infant in your cradle for Aegisthus! Who
did Aegisthus kill?

JENNY: It is written in his journal that it was Orestes!

ORESTES: Nooooo!

SALLY: Of course not.

JENNY: Into whose infant skull did Aegisthus crash his sword!

(ORESTES *is trying to write all this down.*)

BECKY: It is written that your mother killed your father to avenge the death of your sister, Iphigenia.

ORESTES: My sister is dead?

JENNY: It is said your mother wanted to screw Aegisthus!

ORESTES (*to* JENNY): Who is Aegisthus?

JENNY: It is said that she lusts only after political power for herself!

SALLY: It is claimed Aegisthus is a man she can rule. It is said that he is a man she worships.

ORESTES: Who is he? I don't know who he is.

BECKY: Your father is dead. Kill his killers.

SALLY: If you hurt your good mother, your brain will rot and blacken with sores.

JENNY: You must avenge your father or scales will close your eyes and blacken your brain with sores.

ORESTES: I can't write this fast.

BECKY (*handing him books as she goes*): Read these books. It's so beautiful here in the park.

SALLY (*handing him more books as she goes*): Read these books. It's so lovely here in the park.

JENNY (*piling more books in his arms as she turns and, with the others, leaves*): Read these books in the lovely, beautiful park.

(*As* ORESTES *is left with his pile of books and flowers around his neck, he tries to study.* THE SPEAKER, *having observed all this, steps closer to him.*)

THE SPEAKER: Every day we live, Orestes, we learn more and more. We know things we did not know for millions of years about the height of the universe; life on the largest moon of Saturn is possible; we know of transistor radios, cars, and how the lobes of our brains, when photographed, seem netting or moonscape. We know of the biochemical compounds in the fluids of our brains.

ORESTES (*hurling the books down on the floor*): This is written, that is written. Who is doing all this writing? I must talk to someone! (*He kicks a book.*) Yet I must remain calm. I will remain calm. For it is my belief that the truth, if pursued with patience, reveals itself. It is my belief that there are great good lessons in the sky, and the wise know them while all others struggle throughout their lives to move toward some understanding of these great good lessons. I will move toward them. (*He packs his books into the book bag.*) I will move to find them, to find my sister, Electra. She is here. She has been here while Father and Iphigenia are dead. There has been much pain and ruin without me. But where will I find her? Which way shall I go? (*He looks about a little puzzled.*) That way . . . or . . . that way . . . ? (*Pause: He thinks.*) I don't know what way any way is. (*And then, with great exhilaration, he points to his right.*) That way! I feel it!

(*Off he goes as* PYLADES *comes rushing in from behind him.*)

PYLADES (*yelling*): You! You!

(ORESTES *stops and turns back toward* PYLADES, *who looks around furtively.*)

Come here. I have something for you.

(*As* ORESTES *starts back,* PYLADES *moves to meet him.*)

I have found these locks of hair upon the grave of Agamemnon. Do you know them? They are the colors of your own.

ORESTES: I am looking for his daughter.
PYLADES (*taking a piece of parchment from his pocket*): This message is for his son.
ORESTES: I'm very busy.
PYLADES (*conspiratorially*): Are you friend enough to read?
ORESTES (*turning to leave*): I haven't time for any more reading! I've been reading and reading! I've too many questions!
PYLADES (*grabbing* ORESTES, *shoving the paper into his hands*): LOOK AT THIS!

(*And then the voice of* ELECTRA *is heard. She is on the scaffolding behind the cargo net.*)

ELECTRA: Orestes, they keep me in little light!

ORESTES: It is addressed to me. Who sent this? Who is kept in little light?

ELECTRA (*her hands wrapped in the links of rope like the bars of a cage as* ORESTES *scans the note*): High above the city streets I am in jail. I am looking at a flaw near the corner that is like a pockmarked face. The walls of the cell are gray.

ORESTES: I have no friends in jail.

PYLADES: She is in jail.

ORESTES: Who?

PYLADES: Electra.

ORESTES: My sister? She is a princess.

PYLADES: Two days ago there was a great gathering on a hillside in the park. There was a platform with Aegisthus upon it.

ORESTES: Was that two days ago?

PYLADES: Did you see? Were you part of the mob?

ORESTES: No, no. I was in the park to do my reading—I was studying under a tree. I have so many books. An important man was making speeches. Foolish people went running forward at him, screaming, throwing rocks and eggs. I told them to stop; it was terrible.

PYLADES: Electra was among them; your sister was arrested for befouling the name of Aegisthus.

(ORESTES *is horrified.*)

ORESTES: But the only girl among them spit at me.

PYLADES: She was the only girl among them.

ORESTES: She ran to me where I stood. "Pretend I'm with you," she said. Guards were running up. "No," I told her. "You take your punishment. I saw what you did." She spit at me. Could she have been Electra and not known I was Orestes?

(JENNY *comes running in to hand another message to* PYLADES.)

PYLADES: You did not know she was Electra. And you have another message.

ORESTES: What?

ELECTRA (*standing, pressing against the net*): Aegisthus fears me. He fears that I will seduce some guard and lie in secret with him, that I will deliver a son possessed of the rage of our father buried without libations. I take men into the dark corners of this place. I whisper. I hold—I fuck them until they scream. But I know I can not conceive.

(AEGISTHUS *enters carrying a stool,* CLYTEMNESTRA ONE *and* CLYTEMNESTRA TWO *both with him wearing royal gowns. He has a suitcoat over his net toga, medallion and T-shirt.*)

It is my only cry. Nothing happens but that the guards all hurry off to tell one another what Electra has done to them.

AEGISTHUS (*standing atop the stool, begins to speak in the manner of a politician among cronies as* ORESTES *receives and reads a newspaper*): Sometimes I have fun. I have so much fun. I get drunk and go to Agamemnon's grave. I jump all over it. Up and down. I kick the dirt. I piss upon it.

ELECTRA (*screaming at* AEGISTHUS): Abomination!

AEGISTHUS (*laughing, happy*): Aegisthus!

ELECTRA: Murderous adulterer!

AEGISTHUS (*happy, laughing as* ORESTES *is very confused, another messenger running up to him*): Aegisthus! Aegisthus!

ORESTES (*rejecting this last message, he turns to* PYLADES): What is all this reading and reading? Are there no people? This is not enough.

(*He throws down the papers.*)

PYLADES: I will take you. I will show you. Follow me. Follow me!

(*And he grabs the startled* ORESTES *and leads him to the right and they duck, they weave. They press against a wall in shadows.*)

Shhhhhhh. Wait here. You can speak to her through the bars.

(*Looking up to the scaffolding where* ELECTRA *sits brooding, he calls quietly.*)

Electra. I have Orestes with me.

(ORESTES *moves to where he can see* ELECTRA *and she can see him.*)

ELECTRA (*pressing against the ropes*): You have abandoned me.

ORESTES: No.

ELECTRA: I forgive you.

ORESTES: I haven't abandoned you!

ELECTRA: A daughter loves a father, a son a mother, and so you abandon me.

ORESTES (*straining up to be nearer to her*): My interest is justice—goodness—virtue and understanding. I will be fair.

ELECTRA: Is it fair that I sit in jail? Is it good, is it virtuous? Is it just?

PYLADES: You have been away, Orestes. What do you know, living as you did in wealth and exile, while your sister was a slave to Aegisthus, mending clothes, polishing plates?

ELECTRA: Mother must die!

ORESTES: What?

ELECTRA: Only in Mother's death is there hope!

ORESTES: No, no, I disagree, I—

ELECTRA: Think of our poor, good father struggling always for honor and virtue in our land and they butcher him. Our mother and Aegisthus slaughter him!

ORESTES: There is some question of who did what to—

ELECTRA: I was there!

ORESTES: I have a plan; it is my own. I am not as rash as you.

ELECTRA: I am Electra!

ORESTES: I will go to the marble statue of Aegisthus in the park, where the flag of Clytemnestra waves before the temple on which the ideals of our land are carved. I will destroy the flag of our mother; I will shatter the stone likeness of Aegisthus. Upon the monument to the ideals of our land which they have abandoned, I will put flowers.

ELECTRA: What good will that do?

ORESTES: Just wait and see! You'll be surprised!

ELECTRA: Because you want ideals, you think you must perform in that same manner which is to not perform at all. You do nothing!

ORESTES (*moving backward in frustration*): I have only just arrived, but you act like—

ELECTRA: You think to speak in subtle signs and gestures when they are blunt, crude people!

ORESTES: She is my mother.
ELECTRA: Because of you I am locked away!

(*Angrily she strains against the ropes that cage her.*)

ORESTES: I didn't know that was you in the park.
ELECTRA: My degradation is a price I pay to you.
ORESTES: I'll get you out!

(*Reaching to touch her hands with his, he stretches; she crouches.*)

ELECTRA (*pleading, demanding*): Free me!
ORESTES: I will, I will. I promise!

(*He pivots away, and sees on an upper level the large statue of* AEGISTHUS *that has been lying on its side, now being raised.* ORESTES *pulls his sword.*)

I will break into the mind of Aegisthus and sweep aside the ignorance encrusting his heart and soul, which are not unlike my own, for we are both men, both human!

AEGISTHUS (*taking the microphone from* THE SPEAKER *and talking into it, while* ORESTES *scurries to the scaffold and the statue*): One of the things most necessary at the moment is a decision as to whether or not to start higher rediscount rates or begin the sale of our royal securities.

ORESTES (*sword poised above the head of the statue*): Aegisthus, my message for you is as follows: With the shattering of this stone, I will break into your mind. You are a petty, shameful man who has brought corruption all through our land. In your heart you know this. You long for confession and expiation. In the shattering of this statue you will see your shame and guilt and ruin revealed. You will understand my purpose, goodness, and seriousness. You will thank me and beg my help.

(ORESTES *smashes his sword into the head of the statue, as a* MESSENGER *runs up and hands a document to* AEGISTHUS. ORESTES *confronts the shattered statue.*)

What do you have to say to me?
AEGISTHUS: Vandalism is spreading all across our land. Sacrilege. Wanton, petty, psychotic vandalism.

(ORESTES *is pushing the statue over.*)

THE SPEAKER: (*leaning in to use the microphone in Aegisthus' hand.*) You do not know the word "psychotic."

(*The statue topples now.*)

AEGISTHUS: It is everywhere! Sick, demented people are going about destroying the beautiful, wonderful shrines to our wisdom and virtue all across the land.

(*As a message is delivered to* AEGISTHUS.)

ORESTES (*standing over the fallen statue*): Free my sister!
PYLADES AND OTHERS: Free Electra!
AEGISTHUS: This is the work of Electra!

(*And* PYLADES *comes dashing on with a document for* ORESTES.)

PYLADES: Orestes! Orestes! He wars against the Persians—he diverts our resources into a pointless struggle with the Peloponnesians. He slaughters the Vietnamese.
ORESTES: Who are they?
PYLADES: Good, gentle people! He burns their villages.

(ORESTES *comes down to join* PYLADES.)

AEGISTHUS (*to* THE SPEAKER): In addition, who are these people the notes left by the vandals all say I am slaughtering?
THE SPEAKER (*taking back the microphone*): The Vietnamese.
AEGISTHUS: Oh, yes! Slaughter them!
ORESTES (*standing, talking to* PYLADES): In what I have done to his statues and flags, does he not see his crimes? Does he not know that I, Orestes, am here? How can he not see his rotten soul crumbling in the dust of his shattered symbols?
PYLADES: I have heard he intends to cut off Electra's hands.
ORESTES: Cut off—but she is locked away, she—
PYLADES: He feels that if she has no hands, no guard nor any man will want her.
ORESTES: It is not possible.
AEGISTHUS: Cut off Electra's hands. I want her to have no hands, so that the desecration of my wonderful institutions will stop.

(ELECTRA *screams as another messenger comes running up to* PY-LADES.)

ORESTES: What has happened to my sister? I must go to her!

PYLADES (*still reading*): Aegisthus has ordered that her tongue be made so she will never speak. He is going to cut her tongue from her mouth.

ORESTES: What?

PYLADES (*handing him the note*): With no hands or tongue, he says she will inspire no further destruction of his statues.

(ELECTRA *screams, collapsing to the floor.*)

ORESTES: No, no.

(*At the same time,* JENNY, SALLY, *and* BECKY *enter and cower against the scaffolding before* AEGISTHUS.)

How is this possible?

AEGISTHUS: There are crowds of people each night below the windows of my jails. I have many, many jails.

(CLYTEMNESTRA ONE *and* CLYTEMNESTRA TWO *are strolling toward him.*)

ORESTES (*to* PYLADES): Who's that? Who's talking?

PYLADES: Shhhhhhhh. We must hide. Bow down. It is Aegisthus.

(*Trying to pull* ORESTES *to kneel amid the cowering people.*)

ORESTES: What?

PYLADES (*forcing* ORESTES *down as* AEGISTHUS *begins, grandly, to speak*): Bow down. Be still.

AEGISTHUS: When you put one person in jail, another one appears in the street below. It's an equation. And they are all such odd ruined people below our jails—drunkards—foreigners, dwarfs—gathered in the streets. Now they are quiet, bowing down to me as you can see, but often they yell to one another of their lasting love—all accents and foreign words—they are indecent calling up and down. If that report that Orestes is yet alive should be true, I hope he has been sometimes among them, calling up to mute, despairing Electra. She would stare at me in fury and outrage and I would smile, going on about my business, cutting out her tongue. Call out to her, Orestes.

(*And then, whimsicality in his voice, he turns to* CLYTEMNESTRA ONE *and* CLYTEMNESTRA TWO *and gestures toward the sky.*)

See that twinkling star—have you any wishes? I have many wishes. It is—isn't it—the first star. Oh, yes. Let us all wish quickly.

(*As both* CLYTEMNESTRA ONE *and* TWO *cuddle with* AEGISTHUS.)

ORESTES: Who's that with him?

PYLADES: Clytemnestra.

ORESTES: But she embraces him, she kisses him—the man who killed my father.

PYLADES: It's your mother.

ORESTES (*he leaps out screaming as* PYLADES *tries to restrain him*): You will not escape your crimes, Aegisthus!

PYLADES: Run! Now you've done it!

ORESTES: Whore! You whore!

AEGISTHUS: Who is that down there! Who is this criminal who speaks to me of crimes?

ORESTES: You heard me!

PYLADES: Run! With me. Please! RUN!

AEGISTHUS (*bellowing*): Guards. Some vile revolting criminal accuses me of crimes!

PYLADES (*fleeing*): Now!

AEGISTHUS: Guards!

(ORESTES *and* PYLADES *flee as a strobe light flashes on, the light shattering the images of moving people*—BECKY, JENNY, SALLY, PYLADES, ORESTES, *and* THE GIRL—*who all dash about while* AEGISTHUS *paces, receiving messages, reading them, gesturing in one direction and the another while the Speaker's voice, amplified by her microphone, goes on.*)

THE SPEAKER: Strange indeed are objects at apparent rest upon the earth, for they are like beads of water upon a spinning wheel. So long as they spin slowly gravity holds them in place. It is, for example, a little-known fact that objects at the earth's equator are kept moving continually at rather more than one thousand miles per hour. Should we ever find ourselves spinning faster— say, sixteen times our present speed so that we had an eighty- five-minute day—how we would have to hurry, getting up, off to work, eating, playing, back to bed—we should, in addition, see the surprising spectacle of all objects at the earth's equator, winging off on tangents into outer space, the sea and air, of course, accompanying them on their new adventure.

AEGISTHUS: What do you mean you can not find him? He must be destroyed!

(*He stops pacing under the booth and hurls the message into the air, as the strobe cuts out and* ORESTES *bursts out from under the scaffolding with* PYLADES.)

ORESTES: What are we running for? I'm sick of it. I don't care. I am Orestes. I want to know what happened. What am I to do?

(*As* PYLADES *tries to pull him on, he refuses.*)

My sister is in jail. Some stranger is Aegisthus. Some stranger is my mother. You say! Who the hell are you? I must speak to my sister and she has no tongue. I was a child. I must learn who saved me. Did my mother in fact kill my father? What's going on? Why did he kill Iphigenia? I have nothing to work with but the names of the dead. Iphigenia! Agamemnon!

(THE FIGURE *steps out.*)

THE FIGURE: I am here, Orestes, if you wish to speak to me.
PYLADES: Apollo.
ORESTES: Who?
PYLADES: It's Apollo. Called Delian, called Pythian. Called Delian because of Delos, the isle of his birth. Called Pythian for his battle with a serpent, called Phoebus meaning shining, called Lycian meaning wolf-God. Call Sminthian for mouse-God, the God of mice.
THE FIGURE (*to* ORESTES): But whether because I protect mice or destroy them, no one knows.

(*As a number of other* FAMILY MEMBERS *enter.*)

We are friendly people. We roam the hills, all strangers yet we live as a family.

ORESTES (*to* THE FIGURE): Where have you been? I know you.

(*He looks at the others.*)

I know you all.

THE FIGURE (*poking at Orestes' bags and books*): What is all this? You have so many books, Orestes.

ORESTES (*rooting through his books, documents*): My notes. Papers. A journal of what I learned about my life, which I'm trying to understand. My mother, my father, and Aegisthus, who mutilates my poor sister.

THE FIGURE: Tell Aegisthus of his crimes and he will call you "criminal"!

ORESTES: He has already done that.

THE FIGURE (*as* BECKY, SALLY, *and* JENNY *gather around them*): How can words affect a man who thinks he is the source of all meaning? Once you say something to him, he simply takes it, makes it his own and says it back to you? Do you want these girls? They'll do whatever you want.

(THE GIRLS *all laugh.*)

Are you hungry? We have food. You must be hungry.

ORESTES: Yes.

THE FIGURE (*to* JENNY, *who rises and hurries off*): Bread and wine.

(*And back to* ORESTES.)

You should rest. We roam the hills.

ORESTES: Have you cheese?

THE FIGURE: Three kinds.

(BECKY *hands the cheese to* ORESTES, *as* THE FIGURE *is lighting up a hashish pipe.*)

Would you care to smoke?

PYLADES: I would.

(*They all laugh.*)

THE FIGURE (*passing the pipe to* ORESTES): It is a pleasant weed.

(ORESTES *merely puffs.*)

BECKY: You must draw it deep.

(ORESTES *tries.*)

THE FIGURE: I have yearned to meet you for so long, Orestes.
ORESTES (*releasing the smoke*): What do you mean?
THE FIGURE: I have been awaiting you.
ORESTES: You knew of my coming?
THE FIGURE: There is in me a feeling of kinship for people of the
    spirit. Are you not such a creature?
ORESTES: I am looking to understand certain things that have been
    so far very difficult to understand.
THE FIGURE: Son of man, I am the issue of your dreams; Apollyon,
    of the pit. Do with me as you will.
ORESTES: What?
THE FIGURE: It is all in your eyes.

(*He rises suddenly and moves to exit.*)

I shall sing for you and know your heart and you will be in my
army.

ORESTES: What? What did you— Wait! I would like to talk to you
more.

(*He turns back to the group.*)

Where did he go?

BECKY: He'll be back.
PYLADES (*to* ORESTES): I used to be like you. Sometime. Way back.
ORESTES: That makes no sense to me. I am unique.

(*They all laugh. As* BECKY *snuggles up to him,* ORESTES *smiles.*)

I'm planning a lecture series soon—that's what I've decided. It's
our best hope—I must go about the land, trying to wake the
people up, delivering what I know that no one else knows. "What
is the basis on which people do brutal cruel things to one an-

other? And how can it be stopped?" I'm going to make my thinking very clear.

SALLY (*she settles onto the floor at* ORESTES' *feet*): It's a serious,
important question.

ORESTES: In all my reading there was one unforgettable thing more
haunting than all the others. It is the riddle I must come to know.
Though I read scholarly tomes, I found this in a diary. A father
and daughter went into a desert seeking to collect lovely flowers
that grew only in that locale. And then in the confusion of so
much similarity they lost their way. He returned alone. Quite
calm. Perhaps a trifle confused. And he said, and these are his
exact words, "The last I saw of her, she was about two hundred
yards behind me and she was calling, but I couldn't understand
her words. I waved and pointed out the direction in which she
should go. She'll be along in a minute." They found her dead the
next morning, curled at the base of a dune where, at a certain
time each day, there must have been shade.

BECKY: Wow.

ORESTES: How could such a thing have happened?

PYLADES: And now you've let your sister suffer in jail, though she
begged your help. She's lost her hands and had her tongue cut
out, while you did nothing.

THE FIGURE: I have mushrooms.

(*He steps in.*)

ORESTES: What?

THE FIGURE: Mushrooms—red and white. Known from all time.
We eat them, Orestes.

THE SPEAKER: *Amanita muscaria*—clinically proven to bear a
hallucinatory power.

THE FIGURE (*to* ORESTES): They bear a visionary power. Ants seem
huge as trees. Would you not like to see the light and color of
sound streak off your fingers?

SALLY: They enhance everything.

(PYLADES *and the other* GIRLS *laugh.*)

THE FIGURE: Releasing the ether of your soul.

(*Giving* ORESTES *a mushroom.*)

PYLADES: The purest taste of God's seed upon the earth.
ORESTES: What is ether?
THE FIGURE: You. Me, Orestes. Our great capacity is let loose.

(ORESTES *looks at the others smiling at him, and he pops the mushroom into his mouth.*)

We are the finest ether, Orestes, entangled through some accident in this catastrophic gore. The mushroom puts all bone and skin to sleep. We escape. We flee.

(*Music, airy and strange, begins.*)

BECKY: It's true.
THE FIGURE: She knows.

(As BECKY *kisses* ORESTES *and they fall into an embrace on the ground.* THE FIGURE *begins to sing.* PYLADES *begins to kiss one of the other girls.*)

> The trees beyond the sky
> Have a mushroom's glitter
> Each leaf an eye
> And each eye a star
> To see the sun and see the moon,
> To see the sun and see the moon
> To see the sun and kiss Apollo's gentle loving finger.

(*The lyric is repeated, and then the song quietly ends. They all lie there, quietly, looking at the sky. The mood is that of people around a campfire.*)

ORESTES: I thought I would say the things I knew in my heart, and all men, possessed in some secret way of a heart not unlike my own, would hear me and nod as if they had merely forgotten goodness and I had reminded them. Do not the evil know what they are? I believe now they don't and their hearts are as strange to me as stones.
THE FIGURE (*rising to stand over* ORESTES): On such a pleasant, dear sweet evening, would you not like to wipe your hand across the world and find the insect of Aegisthus taken from the air?

(*He snatches at the air.*)

ORESTES: It is obscene that a creature such as he and I are both called human.

THE FIGURE: You are his opposite.

ORESTES: Why is power always possessed by such ugly, arthritic hands?

THE FIGURE: They envy you, Orestes.

ORESTES: No.

THE FIGURE: They have blunted your sister's hands and tongue.

ORESTES: Out of envy?

PYLADES: She had a beauty equaled only by your own.

THE FIGURE: And on another evening, would you not like to wipe your hand again across our world and find your mother gone, a spot of empty air?

ORESTES: I don't think my mother should be—

PYLADES: It's what she deserves—her and your father and Aegisthus, too, sending us off to that goddamn war. After a couple a months, I was deranged, man. We were all deranged. So we went into this village, nobody knew if it was the right one or the wrong one, because there was this village on our maps called one name, but that wasn't what the people living there called it. They called it something I can't pronounce. But we went in shooting because it was an enemy stronghold on our maps and there was this one old lady, I remember, and everybody was shooting her, you could see the bone chips flying in the air. And there was this girl with this baby, so some of the guys fucked her and killed her. It was heavy, man, fillin' up these ditches with bodies; we had to stop to eat lunch.

ORESTES: She has to suffer. My mother—that's what I'm saying. I have a plan to do a painting of her death that will terrorize her— it's going to be a drawing in cruel, hurting detail. I'll write a poem of all my hate of her.

THE FIGURE: BUT SHE MUST KNOW NOTHING! Her slack, broken skin—she is the abomination—Clytemnestra—running back beyond Aegisthus to the hands of your father, corrupted into murdering infants.

ORESTES (*kneeling, groping for his bag, his notes*): No, no, I have
letters—diaries—all here.
(*He waves them.*)

I've cross-checked and there's documented proof that it was not
Arsinoe or Gellissa who saved me. It was my mother. Or
Laodomaia. Laodomaia is a possibility. And regarding my father's
murdering of infants—the accounts all show he fought difficult,
dangerous campaigns—no doubt some child one time or the
other—

(THE FIGURE *snatches the book from Orestes and snaps it shut.*)

THE FIGURE: Do you think both lies and bread are real?
ORESTES: I'm trying to straighten you out, Apollo! Now right here
in file 47 A, I have—

(*as he digs out a file*)

—a letter in which Helen begs my father to help rescue her from
Troy.

THE FIGURE: Helen was a whore and they called her honor—and
goodness, just like your mother. Those papers have put your
sister into agony. Do you want to keep her there? They feed you
lies, I feed you bread.

(PYLADES *puts the bread into The Figure's hand.*)

I have the bread! Do you want the bread?

(*Shoving bread into his mouth.*)

Or do you think the tribes your father conquered paid him
tribute because he was a dear, kind man?

(ORESTES *has become preoccupied with his hand.*)

ORESTES: What?
THE FIGURE: They were king and queen of theft and carnage!
ORESTES: My hand . . . is odd . . .
PYLADES: It is the mushroom.

(*He rises, takes the stool, and exits.*)

ORESTES: No. It is my hand. It has no skin.

THE FIGURE: Even she was a thing he pillaged and stole, and she welcomed it.

ORESTES: I can't think anymore! But there's doubt, I know, about the way they got together in that courtyard. I've read it, and her handmaiden's diary contradicts his soldiers' letters, so that—

THE FIGURE: I was there, Orestes, Apollo in that smoking courtyard, peering up from her I saw his cruelty, the murder in his look as he flung the child, and down from him I saw her wanton eyes begging for his body upon her, I saw his joy at conquest, her wonder at being taken, his simple soldier's heart. I saw the infant float with a startled look, a brief pleasure at his flight until the fabric of his skull crumbled. She drew him down; he took her like a dog. Or do you say that an infant hitting stone is a warrior? Or do you think the enormous wealth of this land all came since Aegisthus or from such goodness? Has it ever been that any land ever had such power because of goodness, because of virtue?

ORESTES (*only interested in his hands now*): I have no hands; is that good or bad?

THE FIGURE: I am sickened that men go on and on believing motherhood most perfect. A seed is planted in a swamp—is that to the credit of the swamp and gore of a woman's belly that goes on wet and futile until a man enters seed to give it purpose? Are we never separate? The tree grown tall struggles toward the lightened sky from which it fell, in which its loving father lives. Only women love this dank cruel place! I have a madness on this point.

(ORESTES *goes for his notes, crawling away from* THE FIGURE.)

You gesture to the air. She is a fungal place. Destroy her, Orestes, or I will make you outcast. I will make your flesh rot upon you like the ruin of age come in a single day. It is my curse. I am your friend, but it is my curse. Do you want my curse? I will take you to the sky.

(ORESTES *is flipping through his books, which he protects from* THE FIGURE.)

ORESTES: I can't read my notes. Where is section II-A, page . . . ? I can't read them.

(*He hugs his notes and books to his chest.*)

I don't feel well, and I can't read . . . I dare not hurt my good mother.

THE FIGURE: All that you are is your father's. Only your body is hers. What is Orestes? Nothing more than the simple swamp of his flesh? Or a man—a creature of air and ethics, aware beyond bone limits!

ORESTES: I will be punished if I do injustice.

THE FIGURE: No, no, you are too young, too beautiful. Take my hand.

(*Dropping his books,* ORESTES *swoons and* THE FIGURE *catches him.*)

ORESTES: I dare not hurt my good mother.

THE FIGURE (*cradling* ORESTES, *easing him to the ground*): You go about fearful of corruption, and power. You think you are innocent, yelling at the air, believing that you are ordained and extraordinary. I will make you real, Orestes. I will make you real. The murderers of Agamemnon die at the hands of Orestes.

(ORESTES *sleeps.*)

Through the blood of the father to the hand of the son, falls the sword.

(*Fits the knife into Orestes' hand, starts to leave.*)

What goes around, comes around.

THE SPEAKER: No longer is it thought that when a weary man collapses into bed, he goes into a firm and restful state. But rather, modern science has learned by attaching electrodes and an electroencephalograph to his scalp, forehead, chin, chest, and penis, that he tosses and moans.

(CLYTEMNESTRA ONE *and* TWO *each holding a blanket wrapped as an infant in their arms enter, moving toward him.*)

His eyes waggle behind closed lids, he whimpers and struggles, his penis becomes erect, and his heart pounds as rapidly as if running a race.

ORESTES (*popping awake*): I am a bubble. A button on the cloak of Aegisthus. A bubble in the sea. And there are . . . things nearby . . .

(*He is staring warily at* CLYTEMNESTRA ONE *and* CLYTEMNESTRA TWO.)

CLYTEMNESTRA ONE: Orestes.
CLYTEMNESTRA TWO: Orestes.
ORESTES: I do not know if I am talking or thinking.
CLYTEMNESTRA ONE: Thinking.
CLYTEMNESTRA TWO: Talking.
CLYTEMNESTRA ONE: We hold the infant of you in our arms.

(*She is kneeling beside* ORESTES.)

See . . . !

CLYTEMNESTRA TWO (*to the blanket in her arms, her back to* ORESTES *on the ground*): Please don't come as you will and must in time to see a guilt in us equal to the hate you feel.
ORESTES (*to* CLYTEMNESTRA TWO): You must explain who saved me.
CLYTEMNESTRA TWO: We are your mother.
CLYTEMNESTRA ONE: But in no secret place within do we feel unfit to live. Must you come?
CLYTEMNESTRA TWO: Down the dimness toward us even as the infant of you in our arms—stirs—in sleep. Do you see?

(*She bends toward* ORESTES, *kneels to his left side, as* CLYTEMNESTRA ONE *is kneeling to his right. They are putting the blankets like babies into his arms. As he takes up the babies, the knife is left lying on the ground.*)

See him looking toward us, nearly smiling?

ORESTES: Ohhh . . . yes.
CLYTEMNESTRA ONE: Nothing in his eyes but need.

(CLYTEMNESTRA ONE *and* CLYTEMNESTRA TWO *are rising now, retreating.*)

CLYTEMNESTRA TWO: Nothing in his eyes but need.

(ORESTES *is trying to hold the blankets to comfort them as* CLYTEM-
NESTRA ONE *and* CLYTEMNESTRA TWO *retreat.* AGAMEMNON, *in
a state of agitation, has entered behind* ORESTES.)

CLYTEMNESTRA ONE: Need.

CLYTEMNESTRA TWO: Need.

ORESTES: Why are you going? Don't go. We need to know, the
babies and me—who saved us?

AGAMEMNON (*loudly*): Orestes!

ORESTES (*huddling over to protect the babies*): Shhhhhhh! We're
sleeping!

AGAMEMNON: Who is it that sits in my chair? I have told him, "Get
out." All my robes, my rings, accept him. Do they not know that
they are mine?

ORESTES (*moving toward* AGAMEMNON): Who are you?

AGAMEMNON: Avenge me! Give me rest!

ORESTES: I don't know who you are!

AGAMEMNON: They stand about awaiting him. They do not seem to
know that they are Agamemnon's chair and bed; Agamemnon's
horse and courtyard, cart and house.

THE SPEAKER: You don't have a car, Agamemnon!

AGAMENON: Cart! Cart! He has my cart!

ORESTES (*realizing who he is*): Agamemnon! Father, I have been
looking for you! I'm Orestes!

AGAMEMNON: I have been looking for you. I wander with no sail. I
spread my arms, I cup my hands to catch the changing air, but
it eludes me. What will take me from this place? I must have
wind.

(*Trying at Orestes' blankets.*)

Are those my sails?

ORESTES (*protecting the babies*): No, nooo! They are babies of me
wrapped in blankets and sound asleep. We're all asleep.

AGAMEMNON: What is this place? I hate this place! What is it that
you want that you brought me here? I don't know where I am.
Once I picked up the drawing of my knee and thought it was the
map of the ocean to Troy. I studied it for hours. Do I now sail it?
Is this place my knee? Do I sail my knee? WAIT!

(*His hand probes the air.*)

Did you feel it? A call. A cry of air.

(*He starts to go, as if following a current of air.*)

ORESTES (*running to him, stopping him*): You must tell me what happened. I don't know what happened.

AGAMEMNON: Your mother stabbed my benevolence; she cut open my innocence. She murdered my virtue.

ORESTES: Do you know what you're saying—what you're talking about?

AGAMEMNON: Avenge me!

(*Suddenly, he pummels the blankets, struggling to take them from* ORESTES *and hurl them to the ground.*)

Avenge me!

ORESTES: Stop it!

AGAMEMNON: Or you are no son of mine!

ORESTES (*falling to his knees to comfort and re-form the babies, while* AGAMEMNON *stands there looking down at him*): Oh, babies, poor babies. Has he hurt you? Where are you?

AGAMEMNON: Kill her! Kill her!

ORESTES: Poor, poor babies, don't listen. Don't worry. I can not hurt my good mother for such a man. No more than could the weeds and nettles and daisies and dandelions rise up and slay the earth because he commands them too. Don't fear, Sweet Earth.

(*He holds the refolded blankets in one arm. With the other hand, he strokes the earth beneath him.*)

Sweet Earth, have I babies of me in my arms? Or are these blankets in which I sleep? Oh, Earth, do you know my mother? As you have cradled the seeds of trees and wheat, roses and clover my good mother cradled me in her center, as rich and grand and deep as you, I can not hurt her.

(*Looking up, sees his father glaring at him.*)

Father, I can not hurt her. From her I must rise to stand like you. Teach me a sport. We will play and have dinner.

(*He rises up to try and emulate his father.* CLYTEMNESTRA ONE *and* TWO *are moving toward him.*)

CLYTEMNESTRA ONE: Don't listen to him, Orestes.

CLYTEMNESTRA TWO: Don't look at him. Look at us.

AGAMEMNON: You are a devious whore, a nagging bitch.

ORESTES: No, no; don't talk that way. We are together at last. If only Electra were here. If only Iphigenia were here.

(*And* ELECTRA *and* IPHIGENIA *come running on.*)

ELECTRA: Hello.

IPHIGENIA: Hello.

ORESTES: Electra! Iphigenia.

(*Hugging* IPHIGENIA.)

Oh, happiness. You're alive, Iphigenia.

IPHIGENIA: Yes, yes.

ORESTES (*hugging* ELECTRA): You have your tongue, Electra, you have your hands.

ELECTRA: Of course. I am as mother's womb delivered me into the world, a perfect baby. As she did all of us, Orestes. Each with all our arms and legs, our two ears and eyes, ten fingers, ten perfect toes. Mother's womb was so good to us.

ORESTES (*to* CLYTEMNESTRA ONE *and* CLYTEMNESTRA TWO): Thank you Mother.

ELECTRA AND IPHIGENIA: Thank you, Mother.

ELECTRA: And Father's perfect seed.

ORESTES: Thank you, Father.

ELECTRA AND IPHIGENIA: Thank you, Father.

ORESTES: I love you, Father. What is a man? How am I to be a man?

CLYTEMNESTRA ONE: You are a poem.

CLYTEMNESTRA TWO: A jewel.

AGAMEMNON: It is not easy.

ORESTES: You look angry, Father. No, no, don't be angry. I will make you happy.

(*As* ORESTES *moves toward his father,* CLYTEMNESTRA ONE *and* TWO *both groan.*)

CLYTEMNESTRA ONE: No.

CLYTEMNESTRA TWO: Come here.

ORESTES: Don't worry, Mother. It's all right. Please. There is nothing to fear. It is only the mushroom.

(*He is hastening about, gathering them all, organizing them.*)

We are a family separated for too long, and now we have come together and we must stay together. Our blood runs back to Tantalus, but we are not like him. No, no, we move away from him, up from him. We progress. We advance so far away he is unknown, the other end of time. Not kind and good as we, his eyes are mean. But we are no longer like him. We must simply stay together and think one slow thought: "We are not going mad. We are not going mad."

(*He has brought them all together, his arms embracing their four heads in a row. He is trying to teach them, and they are trying to repeat the lesson, repeating by rote without inflection.*)

AGAMEMNON AND CLYTEMNESTRA ONE AND TWO AND IPHIGENIA AND ELECTRA: We move away from him, up from him, we progress.

(*They are overlapping and repeating as is* ORESTES *as he moves backward from them, while facing them, preparing to take a photo of them. The camera flashes and* AGAMEMNON *breaks away to pick up the knife that* THE FIGURE *put into Orestes' hand.*)

AGAMEMNON: What's this? I don't know what this is.

ORESTES: What? No, no.

(*Running to them.*)

To cut the bread. To cut the bread.

AGAMEMNON: To cut the bread?

ORESTES: It is a picnic we are on, and that's to cut the bread and cheese. Here is the bread. I have the bread.

(*Holding up the bread.*)

Is this not the bread?

(*As* IPHIGENIA *suddenly yelps with pain and leaps back from her father, who has thrust at her with the knife.*)

ELECTRA: He cut me. Father cut me.
ORESTES: No, Father.

(*Taking the knife and throwing it down onto the floor.*)

Stop it.

AGAMEMNON: I didn't.
ORESTES: I won't stand for that, Father.

(*As* CLYTEMNESTRA TWO *leaps to pick up the knife.*)

AGAMEMNON: Watch out for her!
ORESTES: Mother, give that to me.

(*Moving to her, taking the knife.*)

Please. We must be careful with this thing. Look at what happened to Father. Look at what happened to Iphigenia. And they have said that I am to kill you, Mother, though I don't want to. Out of love for him, whom I have never actually seen. Yet they say I will. Because you abandoned me. Is that why? Did you send me yowling in my little cradle into endless exile away from you? If so, then duty to Father is an alibi. Or do I simply wish to wipe from the world what your body says about my own—we grow old. Do I yelp up at you even now from that cradle in which you put me down never to lift me? Is hatred then my motive, love my excuse? Apollo says you murder infants—you put them into the hands of men who break their little heads on swords and walls, and I must kill you, or his curse would ruin me with the plague of age in a single day. Is fear of him then my motive, hate of you my alibi, duty my excuse? You must tell me. I have a knife in my hand and I—they say—will pierce you with it, Mother!

(*During this tirade, the "family portrait" has broken apart. Now* PYLADES, *carrying a telescope, is coming up behind* ORESTES.)

What is my motive, which my alibi—what is my excuse!?

PYLADES: Look into this to find the answer, Orestes.

ORESTES (*whirling*): I'm fine. I'm doing fine!
PYLADES: Have another mushroom.

(*As* ORESTES *takes the telescope.*)

ORESTES (*scolding* PYLADES): Forgive me.

(*Behind* ORESTES, *the neglected family members are going off in different directions.*)

ORESTES: Your words are bubbles, your bubbles float in the air. I hear in my ear.

(*Starting to look into the telescope, which is pointed directly at the ground.*)

It makes my foot big.

PYLADES: Look in the other end. And have another mushroom.

(ORESTES *turns the telescope around as he lets* PYLADES *put another mushroom into his mouth. He stares down at his foot again.*)

ORESTES: It makes my foot little. Where is my sister?
PYLADES: In the heavens.

(*The phone starts to ring and* ORESTES *looks upward.*)

ORESTES: I see only the stars—I see only the Gods.
PYLADES: Good-bye.
ORESTES (*lowering the telescope, he looks at* PYLADES): It makes you far away.
PYLADES (*starts backing up*): Good-bye.
ORESTES (*watching* PYLADES *through the telescope*): Good-bye. Oh, it makes you further and further away. You are so far away.

(*Turning the telescope away from* PYLADES *and looking around.*)

Oh, it makes everything far away.

(*As he swings the telescope back, looking for* PYLADES, *who has exited.*)

It makes the world far, far away . . .

(*Swinging the telescope on and on. He lowers the telescope.*)

They're all gone. Mother, father, sisters, friend.

(*The phone stops ringing and he looks up.*)

Iphigenia? I thought our father great, but he is a windy fool. Oh, my sister in the heavens, you must tell me what happened. Why our father killed you, and did your spirit move the wind? Did our mother kill our father because of you? Is that not a thing we can understand? I say there are certain things that, if I am to remain a human man, I must not ever cease to know them. What are they? Please tell me! Does no one want to help me? Does no one care what happens to poor Orestes fed so fucking long on bread and dreams he thinks that both are real! How am I to ever begin my lectures? I will never get it clear and I must—the thing that I know that no one else knows, something sufficiently vile and disgusting, so that I may begin my lectures all across this land. How is it possible a father fails a daughter, a son fails a father, a wife a husband. It is all paper.

(*He has begun tearing up his papers.*)

Notes. It is all notes.

(*He throws the pieces high in the air. They fall back toward him and beyond them he sees the hanging Godheads.*)

That float in the air. Below . . . the Gods. My sister is not there. Dear Gods, what in the air holds your head above me that will not hold me? Is there only the air? This journey is too long. God help me—I cannot find a friend. You must speak to me. I can see in your form that you have all wisdom and goodness, yet you tell me nothing, you break my little life. And what is goodness and what is wisdom?

(*Now he is climbing amid the ropes of the cargo net, having reached up to pull himself so he can rise up near the Godheads, straining to get face to face with one of the Godheads.*)

I am here. Cold stony bubbles of eyes, you must think of me and make me other than I am. You must hear me. Rigid icy brain, hear me, see me. Rigid icy brain, you must think of me!

(ORESTES *is face-to-face with the Godhead, his nose almost touch-*
ing, when suddenly there is a figure below him with a masked head
that is white, skull-like, duplicating the hanging Godheads.)

PYLADES: What do you want?

(*And the rest of the* FAMILY MEMBERS *are arriving, all masked in*
white skull-like Godheads. They carry wands that will light and
flash.)

ORESTES: What?
PYLADES: What do you want to know?
ORESTES (*still facing the Godhead*): Do you speak? Do you speak to
  me, Gods?
BECKY: Hello, I'm here.
JENNY: Here.
SALLY: Hello. You called.

(*Startled,* ORESTES *looks down; he sees them.*)

JENNY: You called.
BECKY: Hello. Hello.
ORESTES (*staring in amazement*): What?
BECKY: Don't you know us? Don't you know us?

(*And all yell, "Hello, hello, don't you know us?" They wave.*)

THE SPEAKER: It is not currently known whether consciousness is
  an electrochemical property of the brain or a product secreted by
  the lobes of the brain in the manner that bile is secreted by the
  liver.
BECKY: Climbing to the Gods, you climbed into your brain.
SALLY: We are your thoughts, Orestes. We are your thoughts.
PYLADES: Apollo sent us, God of reason and the pit, called Apollyon.
ORESTES: I am in my brain? Hello!
SALLY: It is the mushroom. Hello!
ORESTES: No. It is my brain. I am in it, Iphigenia! Mother, Father,
  we are in my brain.
PYLADES: Have you ever been elsewhere?

(ORESTES *leaps in joy in the net above the happy figures of his brain,
below the dangling skulls of his gods.* THE SPEAKER *speaks and the
figures of his brain begin to move the flashing wands. The ropes of the
net and the ropes that entwine the set start to glow.*)

THE SPEAKER: Because the activity in the brain is mainly electrical,
an electrochemical change in a single neuron, and there are
some thirteen trillion in the body, institutes a series of changes
all along the nerves so that an electrical impulse flows along its
fibers like a spark along a fuse toward an explosion.

ORESTES (*laughing*): I am in my brain!

ALL: You are in your brain.

ORESTES: I am in my skull; my thoughts have said so. I am seeing
what I am thinking.

(*As high to his right a molecular structure of lights flashes on, and all
the figures of his brain turn and point with their own flashing lights.*)

There! That's my question! How is it possible that a man claim-
ing a father's love for a daughter could leave her alone in a desert
to die?

ALL: How is it possible?

(*And in answer, high to his left, another structure of lights flashes on.
They all point and look.*)

ORESTES: There! He wishes to live and believes she will follow.
Such is the way we let one another die.

ALL: Logically.

ORESTES: Logically. Reasonable conclusions based on a sound and
logical premise based on other conclusions and a still more distant, unremembered premise.

(*More flashing.*)

ALL: It's the structures.

ORESTES: The structures.

ALL: Of course.

ORESTES: The myths and structures that are like floodlamps in the
night, and they show you directly where to look while making it

impossible for you to see anything should you look in another direction.

(*His face shimmers in light; the net and set glow and flicker as he points to a new structure.*)

There!

(*They all look to a molecular structure of lights flashing on high to his left.*)

That one. Again.

(*The lights go off and on.*)

That's it! Why Clytemnestra and Aegisthus ought to die—because they believe in the myths that make you blind to all they do not show—they believe in the structures and myths, and so they think that they are sane and civilized, king and queen, with more right to slaughter Electra than I have right to bring killing down on them. I mean, what would it be? What, brain? What, Gods? The measurable difference between motive—

(*And high in front of him another pattern of lights pops on, everyone pointing.*)

alibi—

ALL: —the same—

(*The lights flash and flash.*)

ORESTES: —and excuse. Used, of course, as man applies them to himself and others apply them to him. Nothing! Science doesn't know. Not Pythagoras or Heraclides; they haven't the means.

(*He is leaning forward in the net, and slowly he flips forward, hovers briefly in the air, lands softly on the floor.*)

There is only the air in which we float and talk.

THE GIRL (*gently, wisely*): What goes round comes round, O.
ORESTES: What?

(*And the* FAMILY MEMBERS *are leaving as* THE GIRL *enters to stand behind him.*)

THE SPEAKER: Experimenters have sent out sounds wiggling through the fabric of the air two million miles beyond the moon where reflecting layers bounce them back.

ORESTES (*facing* THE GIRL): Hello.

THE GIRL: What goes around comes around. I mean, what's a moment?

ORESTES: I don't know.

(*He settles beside her.*)

THE GIRL: People make squares where there's only circles in the entire height of God's universe. I mean, have you ever seen a square in the entire height of God's universe?

ORESTES: No.

THE GIRL: It's not your choice. You just do it and you're the thing that does it, see. It won't happen if it isn't s'posed to. It won't happen if it isn't just. I did it, O.

ORESTES: Did what?

THE GIRL: The thing you're worried about. Wearin' my sneakies, which are all black clothes to make it hard to see you in the night, and we wore 'em at first just to get the fear, sneakin' into people's houses, but we was kind when we killed 'em, not tellin' we was gonna kill 'em, so they could go in peace into all eternity.

ORESTES: You killed people?

THE GIRL: We broke into this house and I looked into the rooms and there was this man and woman talkin' so I tole Tex, "There's this man and woman talking."

ORESTES: You killed people? You already did it?

THE GIRL: There was knives, I know—big—I think, though I can't get any picture in my mind right now.

ORESTES: You're so pretty and you already killed people.

THE GIRL: Long time ago, long time ago.

ORESTES: Oh, wow.

THE GIRL: They were all fancy dressed. There was a guy sleepin' on the floor and Tex told me to tie him up and I very nearly couldn't find any rope the house was so big, I was so nervous, oh,

wow. And Tex says—when they asked what we wanted—"I'm
Lucifer here to do Lucifer's business."

(*Together they laugh a little at this, both smiling, whimsical.*)

And the one on the couch, he's the one who when I hesitated in my
stabbing him, oh, wow, he reached up to get me by the hair and
was pulling so I hadda fight for my life and six or seven times in
self-defense I stabbed him in the leg until Tex shot him. And the
pretty one, she kept talkin' how she wanted to live and have her
baby, when I had her in the headlock—this was before we did the
fancy writing on the walls—and it was so easy, kinda. The other
woman running out the door and getting stopped—"Okay," she
says, "I give up," and puts her hands up and Tex stabs her in the
stomach. And meanwhile the pretty one's so still in my arms.
Ohhh, I went home and I made love, I know I made love. Like I'd
like to make love with you, O. I mean, we went in and we went out
as natural as the wind that took us there. Coyotes howl.

(*She laughs.*)

Aren't we all just natural things in God's world? Is a person less a
natural thing than a hurricane or an earthquake or pneumonia in
the air of God's world? We went in there with knives as natural as
the wind or rain or old age, O. They'da never survived Aulus, or
My Lai, or you, O, or God's earthquakes or floods, anyway. If
they weren't supposed to die, we wouldn'ta been there.

THE SPEAKER: (*indicating* ORESTES, *pointing to various spots on his
head*): At each instant of our lives, some millions of neurons are
firing. The task of the brain is to sort these many impulses,
establish priorities, amid this popping, these explosions.

ORESTES: Oh, I'm free of it—free at last to hate and hate this world
in which I need and believe in honor, tenderness, and love, but
find them nowhere.

(*Rushing to* THE GIRL, *grabbing her.*)

I will say: They are in me. All in me.

THE GIRL: They are, O. They are all in you.

ORESTES: I will say my mother is a whore who knelt in sunlight in
the courtyard of her first young murdered husband.

THE GIRL: That happens sometimes.

ORESTES: As she surrendered her firstborn son into my father's killing hand, so she wished me to die at the hand of Aegisthus. It was Laodomaia who saved me. Good sweet Laodomaia.

THE GIRL: She was a good person. That's such a pretty name.

(*The music has begun.*)

ORESTES: And I see dying only as a good and gracious friend grown as weary as I of my ordeal.

(*Together they sing to the building music, many other voices joining in and enriching them, though they are together and alone.*)

SONG:

We will be a circle in the height of God's universe.
We will be a circle with no edges, no ledges
I am God and I am good Ooooo, Orestes
Circle is my name, circle is my name
We will be a bulb, a skull, a tear, a star, a sack of black air
To shut out the life of my mother
As a clot I will float in the blood of Aegisthus
As a clot I will float in the red and blue tubes of Aegisthus
I will crush his fat heart
I will choke his fat heart
Ooooo Aegisthus!
Ooooo Orestes!

(*In the final whirl and leap of the music,* THE GIRL *and* ORESTES *rush off, as* AEGISTHUS, *in a luxurious dressing gown, enters. He wears dress shoes and socks, but his legs are bare. He strides onto the stage.*)

AEGISTHUS: It's been my goodness—I don't know how long since last I saw good, good Clytemnestra. It was either here or somewhere else. I get confused. It's morning at one time; night at another. It's morning, it's night. I get up, go to bed. "Hello; good night." I sleep, or I don't sleep. I get up. It occurs to me that I should worry, that I haven't eaten, that I am sitting when I'm standing and standing when I'm sitting.

(BECKY, *still wearing the white Godhead, but with a bowler hat upon it, rushes in to deliver a message.*)

Messengers come and go. They deliver and take messages. Sometimes in the deep of the night, I screw a maiden.

(*He laughs a little, nods; proud of this.*)

I screw her pretty good. And there are moments when I am having her I think of Clytemnestra. But sometimes when I was having Clytemnestra, I thought of maidens. I don't know what it all means. It seems I haven't seen Clytemnestra for so long. She could be in the corridor just beyond the wall and she might be gone forever. Who am I to say? It sometimes seems to matter if she's absent, but it rarely seems to matter if she's dead. She's always been absent at one time or another. Is there a difference if she's dead?

(*Another messenger,* JENNY, *who wears the white Godhead mask and a straw hat and scarf, has come running in with another note for him. Handing the note, she flees.*)

The messages say, "No. Maybe." The messengers come and go and tell me of this and that, and off they go. In the corridors of my castle, they scurry about, zipping here and there and back to me to tell me of my stocks and bonds, lungs and liver, the degree of lag between monetary and all other economic changes. It occurs to me that Clytemnestra is in danger. I have dreams of little people breaking her apart.

(*He sees the two Clytemnestras strolling across the scaffolding.*)

Oh, there she is, there she is.

(*They acknowledge him with a nod.*)

So good to see you. I've just been explaining our system. It's going well.

(SALLY *comes dashing in with a message. She wears the white Godhead mask, a top hat, sunglasses, and scarf.*)

And sometimes the word I receive pertains to Orestes. For instance, he just told me Orestes is in the castle. Now what am I to think of that? And even if it's true, how am I to know whether the Orestes of whom he is speaking is the one with whom I am concerned? There are a lot of Orestes.

(*He must correct himself.*)

Or-es-tee-ses. I mean, it's a common name.

(*He smiles, gestures grandly.*)

And the castle is enormous. What room is he in? Does he speak my language? The messenger didn't—didn't—

(PYLADES *is there, wearing a newsboy's cap and whispering into Aegisthus's ear.*)

The most remote wing in the entire castle—way down beneath the basement even—in the tombs and ventricles. What's he doing there? I wonder. I'll have all the trapdoors barricaded. Soon there'll be wolves and antibodies lurking in all the ground-floor halls.

(*And* BECKY *is handing him another note.*)

Well, well. Indeed. No, no, that's nothing to do with Orestes, but rather something to do with a certain portion of my business arrangements that seem to be collapsing. I'll have some of my men to do a little something to reorder it, buoy it up.

(AEGISTHUS *gestures to* PYLADES, *standing off to the side, who turns to face* AEGISTHUS.)

Go tell Michael and Edgar to sell all the fish and buy half back. Tell Russel and Harold to have all the farmers plant carrots.

(*As* PYLADES *goes running off,* JENNY *has hurried on from the opposite direction behind* AEGISTHUS *and is whispering another message.*)

Well, now . . . , she says Orestes has been reported in a closet on the ground floor. I have my doubts about that. I nevertheless suggested that they seal off that area. Little goes on there. There are, after all, whole sections, floors and chambers we scarcely ever use. Having it sealed off is merely a precaution, just as their word of his presence is merely a precaution, just as their word of his presence is merely a report. And what do reports and precautions deal with? Possibilities. So it is possible now that Orestes is in the castle. What's new in that? Hasn't it always been possible?

(BECKY *crosses to* AEGISTHUS *with a note.*)

That's not what I said. That's not what I said. "Sell all and buy half. Sell all and buy half."

(*He throws the note at her.*)

They sold half and bought all, which puts everything right back in the same mess I was trying to rearrange.

(*And already* PYLADES *is there whispering in his other ear.* AEGISTHUS *pushes him away.*)

All right. So what? So he's on the third floor? Who cares. Fuck him. Fuck Orestes. Go fuck yourself, Orestes!

(*By the time he comes back center,* JENNY *has another message for him. He reads it, then backs away from her.*)

He is not. He couldn't be. No. No. There's an entire group of battle-notch-top-crack-big-troops; he couldn't be there. SEAL IT OFF! SEAL IT OFF! BLOCK THE WHOLE THING!

(*Turning, he finds* SALLY *with a note in her outstretched hand. He takes the note, looks at it. She shrugs and exits.*)

What? He is not! He is not. Wouldn't I see him?

(*Warily, he looks about the empty room.*)

He says . . . Orestes . . . is in this room.

(*He looks about again.*)

Must . . . be . . . hiding. Your mother isn't home right now, if she's why you've come! I don't know where she is!

(*Pause; he thinks: he's not afraid.*)

I'm talking to the air. It's not that I'm not afraid because I don't think he'd hurt me if he was here. It's that I don't think he's here. I DON'T THINK YOU'RE HERE, ORESTES.

(*Slight pause.*)

But . . . if you are . . . you can have that side of the room over there . . .

(*Pointing front and backing up.*)

and I'll take this side over here.

(PYLADES *enters, whispers to* AEGISTHUS, *and exits.*)

He says he's not on that side of the room. He's on . . . this . . . on this . . .

(*Moving backward, groping backward for a safe place, his hand contacts a scaffold pole and* JENNY *comes on with a rope and ties his hand to the pole. He looks at her.*)

On . . . this . . . side of the . . . room . . . Well, I'll just go over to that side—

(*As he starts to move, he cannot, his hand bound to the pole. He stares at the rope binding his wrist.*)

I seem to—it seems—I'm all . . . entangled. Oh, well. I'll get out of this in just a minute. Surely. It's nothing at all. I don't feel so badly. I've been in worse spots, a lot worse spots.

(*Pause.*)

Is it because you're invisible that I don't see you? Do you . . . see you . . . , Orestes? I see me. Do you . . . see me?

THE SPEAKER (*walking right up to* AEGISTHUS): Maybe the reason you can't see him, Aegisthus, is because something is interfering with his light rays.

(AEGISTHUS *stares at her.*)

We don't really see one another anyway—what we see is waves of different lengths of light bouncing off us in the shape of us. Maybe his light was ricocheted or something and off it bounced into outer space, and that's why you don't see him. Maybe you'll see him later.

(*She turns, leaves.*)

AEGISTHUS: Will I see you later, Orestes?

(*Pause.*)

Oh, he's here. He is. I know it. We're both here. Oh, I don't—
Orestes—I don't—I've never dealt all that well with people—you
see, it's always been diagrams and—you understand—maps—
papers—letters—if you don't want to speak to me, could you send
me a letter? Could I send you a letter?

(SALLY *comes strolling by.*)

Would you . . . , would you untie my hand? See how it's all—

(*She ties his other hand to the scaffold.*)

No, no. This one over here. This one. Untie. Untie!

(*She exits.*)

No, no. UN! UN!

(*As from above him the letter falls and floats past him.*)

Oh, my goodness . . . the letter.

(THE FIGURE *leaps down from the scaffolding to the floor, as* THE
GIRL *and* ORESTES *push the tub, containing* CLYTEMNESTRA ONE
and CLYTEMNESTRA TWO, *racing in past* AEGISTHUS. *Both of the
Clytemnestras have their hands bound behind them and they are
terrified. They are back-to-back in the tub, and they are blindfolded
and gagged with masking tape.* THE FIGURE *adds a mask or unlooses
his hair and it falls long and black down to his shoulders as he
advances close to* AEGISTHUS.)

THE SPEAKER: That is Abaddon, who is . . .

(*opening the Bible and reading from it*)

". . . the angel of the abyss, whose name in Hebrew is Abaddon,
and in Greek, Apollyon, or the destroyer." Revelations. Chapter
Nine. Verse Eleven.

AEGISTHUS (*to* THE FIGURE): Hello.

(*And* THE FIGURE *leans to Aegisthus' ear and whispers something quickly.*)

But . . . That's impossible. No, no I've got a perfect heart. Absolutely perfect. You didn't read my electrocardiogram or you wouldn't say that. My electrocardiogram is always perfect. Always absolutely perfect. Absolutely one hundred percent per— BULLSHIT!

(*As the Clytemnestras begin crying out in terror behind their gags.*)

THE FIGURE (*to* THE GIRL *and* ORESTES): Let them speak!

(ORESTES *and* THE GIRL *tear the gags off the Clytemnestras.*)

AEGISTHUS: BULLSHIT! BULLSHIT!
CLYTEMNESTRA ONE: What are you doing to my husband?
AEGISTHUS (ORESTES *is whispering into his ear*): BULLSHIT! BULLSHIT!
CLYTEMNESTRA TWO: What are you doing to my husband?
AEGISTHUS: They are calling me pig.
ORESTES (*bellowing at* AEGISTHUS): Rich fucking pig!
AEGISTHUS: They are calling me rich fucking pig!

(THE GIRL *puts a pillowcase over Aegisthus' head.*)

They are putting a hood over my head!
CLYTEMNESTRA TWO: Don't hurt my husband!

(THE GIRL *has a large fork and an apple in her hands.*)

AEGISTHUS: Open the letter! Open the—who did I hurt? I only hurt Agamemnon. Only Agamemnon!
CLYTEMNESTRA TWO: I can't see my husband.
CLYTEMNESTRA ONE: Where is my husband?
AEGISTHUS: I killed you when you were an infant. "Is that him?" I said. Spitting, smelly little thing! I hit you with my sword, Orestes!
ORESTES (*moving near to* AEGISTHUS): Think of yourself as a Vietnamese!
AEGISTHUS: A what? A who?

ORESTES: Think of yourself as a duck, Aegisthus, a squirrel.

AEGISTHUS: No, no. Orestes says he loves everybody, but all his songs are all about himself. Only—

ORESTES (*bellowing*): WE WILL GET IT INTO YOU, ALL PARANOIA!

(AEGISTHUS *shudders in terror, murmuring, "No, no, no," as* THE FIGURE *moves from the end of the tub to stand behind* AEGISTHUS *under the scaffold.*)

THE SPEAKER: How is it now in the moment that we learn that we are insubstantial as a snowflake and of no more consequence? Is it with horror, consolation, tranquillity?

AEGISTHUS: Where is the letter? Read the—

(*As* THE FIGURE, *having snuck up behind* AEGISTHUS *and put his arms around* AEGISTHUS, *squeezes savagely and lifts him upward and backward;* Aegisthus' *legs flail at the air.*)

What, what? What are you doing? Why is this hood over my head? Why have you put this hood over my head? I have no life in this hood! I am a grocer! I run a grocery! I have no life in this hood!

(THE GIRL *jams the apple against the pillowcase and drives it into* Aegisthus' *mouth. He hangs in the air, looking like a pig with an apple in his mouth as* THE GIRL *jams the fork into his heart. His feet kick helplessly at the air as she presses and he tries to breathe.*)

THE SPEAKER: The heart's fantastic powers as a pump add up to a lifetime of amazing statistics. Its job is to keep sixty thousand miles of veins and capillaries supplied. Not made of stone or steel or accessible for constant repair, it is a bundle of living cells, weighing less than a pound and small enough to hold in the palm of the hand.

(AEGISTHUS *cries out in great pain, goes slack in the arms of* THE FIGURE.)

CLYTEMNESTRA ONE: What have you done to my husband?

CLYTEMNESTRA TWO: What have you done to my husband?

THE FIGURE: Is it Agamemnon you mean?

(*As he and* ORESTES *advance on her.*)

ORESTES: Or that other? The first?

THE FIGURE: Do you mean Aegisthus?

CLYTEMNESTRA TWO: What?

CLYTEMNESTRA ONE: What?

ORESTES: Charlie says you are vain. He says you can not understand how you are not important anymore.

CLYTEMNESTRA ONE: You are children.

ORESTES: He says you can not understand that you do not matter, you can not admit that you abandoned my good, brave father for this mediocre, cruel, stupid, little man.

(*Behind them* THE GIRL *is smearing blood from a bowl all over the pillowcase. Plucking the apple from Aegisthus' mouth, she takes a bite.*)

CLYTEMNESTRA ONE: Who are you?

ORESTES: I am Orestes, here to do Agamemnon's business.

(*And he spins the tub and the blindfolded women scream.*)

CLYTEMNESTRA TWO: I saved you!

THE FIGURE: Clytemnestra, you are too rich to have ever been anything but a whore.

CLYTEMNESTRA ONE: You fix your eyes upon me and think that I agree with you. Orestes. No, Nooo!

(ORESTES *moves away, leaving her speaking to the air.*)

In no secret place within have I condemned myself. You don't know how good I feel, and how I still love you. Guilt is not a harsh unbearable thing. You do not know how it is easy. Eas—

ORESTES: And now you seek to pretend innocence before me.

(*His voice behind her startles her. She does not know where he is.*)

CLYTEMNESTRA ONE: No, no, that is nothing. It is nothing that I want, nor did I ever want it or possess or lose it, no matter what I may have thought. He deserved to die. He deserved the death I gave him.

THE FIGURE: Who?

ORESTES: Who's that?

CLYTEMNESTRA ONE: Agamemnon.

ORESTES: Who's talking about Agamemnon?

THE FIGURE: We're talking about the infant.

ORESTES: The one you handed to my father for him to smash against a rock like an old bottle.

CLYTEMNESTRA ONE: I don't know what you're talking about.

ORESTES (*kneeling left of the tub as* THE FIGURE *kneels to the right*): In what part of town did it happen?

THE FIGURE: WHERE?

CLYTEMNESTRA TWO: Dirt.

CLYTEMNESTRA ONE: Dirt. Courtyard.

CLYTEMNESTRA TWO: My husband is a grocer!

CLYTEMNESTRA ONE: My husband is a grocer. My child. I love my child.

CLYTEMNESTRA TWO: No. Help. I love my child.

ORESTES (*seizing* CLYTEMNESTRA ONE *by the hair*): You were in sunlight.

THE FIGURE: You were a pig beguiling him.

ORESTES: A whore beguiling him to do your murder. To make it seem you fought against the hands you guided as a lover, you conspired to kill my innocent father.

(*He puts a hood over her head.*)

CLYTEMNESTRA ONE: Let me have my baby. Iphigenia!

(ORESTES *puts a hood over the head of* CLYTEMNESTRA TWO *and the phone begins to ring and ring and ring.*)

CLYTEMNESTRA TWO (*as* THE FIGURE *drifts away*): Answer, answer . . . !

(ORESTES *takes a knife from the tub. He slits* CLYTEMNESTRA TWO's *throat.*)

CLYTEMNESTRA ONE: Hello.

(ORESTES *slits the throat of* CLYTEMNESTRA ONE, *as across the background the* FAMILY MEMBERS *have drifted, led by* THE GIRL, *all wearing dark ski masks.* ORESTES *is writing "Helter Skeelter"*—

misspelled—on the wall in blood as the others have gathered, kneeling off to the side to face THE GIRL, *who faces out. And the ringing stops and* THE GIRL *smiles at the* FAMILY MEMBERS.)

THE GIRL: So Abaddon says, "Last time was sloppy," and I go, "Okay, no talk about Lucifer tonight."

(*To* ORESTES, *still at the tub, looking in at the bodies:*)

Did you see the pictures of their kids when we came in, oh, wow!

(*Back to* THE FAMILY.)

Maybe they'll come for Sunday dinner and find 'em.

(*They all laugh, and she looks to* ORESTES.)

Want some zu-zu's, O? Okay if I call you "O"?

(*He nods to her, smiles. She throws him a piece of candy that arcs across the space between them. He catches it.*)

When he was tying 'em up, the piggie kept saying how he was a grocer or somethin' and the piggette keeps goin', "What are you doing to my husband?" We didn't say nothing to scare 'em. Just let 'em discorporate, see, 'cause when they scream that's what they carry into infinity. But they were yelling all the same—what could we do?—so we took off real fast after O here writes "Helter Skelter" in blood on the wall, only he misspells it, oh, wow—and I had some chocolate milk in the kitchen. And when we watched the newscast—I went like I was an insane person, jumping and yelling—wow, it really helped me to know all those people we got were so important as they were.

ORESTES (*leaving the knife in the tub, turns to face* THE FIGURE, *who stands near the scaffolding, and the drooping body of* AEGISTHUS): I thought it would take longer . . . be harder.

THE FIGURE (*if he has worn a mask to be Manson, or added costume, or changed his hair, it is all back now, so he is as he started*): You imagined furies would rush upon you. Did you think to hear them screeching as you stood to look around? No, no, it will not happen.

ORESTES: I feel so incredibly good.

THE FIGURE (*moving to the end of the tub*): You have killed your mother and it means nothing and you have seen the nothing that it means.

ORESTES: I do.

THE FIGURE: Of course.

ORESTES: And yet I feel, there should be no more children.

THE FIGURE (*moving farther down*): Orphan! Orphan, what need of children, when you are all, the first and last. I have a golden rope.

ORESTES: A what?

THE FIGURE (*bounding suddenly away and up into the scaffolding*): Come here. Come with Apollo. A golden rope—to take you higher. You would be higher, would you not?

ORESTES: I would, I would.

(*Follows, eagerly, and then he stops.*)

And yet sometimes, Apollo, I look at you and you seem many shells of skin behind which you recede from me to a center I have never seen . . . a hideous lunatic eye.

THE FIGURE: Sometimes you seem exactly that same way to me, Orestes.

ORESTES: I do?

THE FIGURE: Let me raise you up. I want to raise you to the heights.

(ORESTES *moves, onto the net where* THE FIGURE *is pointing.*)

ORESTES (*suddenly erect, facing out,* THE FIGURE *behind him*): And it is my verdict that vile, cunning Agamemnon, noble and cruel, butchered his most sweet and foul Iphigenia, and good Clytemnestra, out of heat and hate, passion and reason, pity and self-deceiving self-revelation, murdered good Agamemnon, and I am innocent.

THE FIGURE: Orestes!

ORESTES (*leaning backward to* THE FIGURE *for support; in a way, giving himself over to* THE FIGURE): Apollo.

THE FIGURE: Apollo and Orestes.

ORESTES (*rising slowly up into the air*): I thought I would be destroyed. I thought I could not kill. I let fear run me all over the world, but I have caressed my demon, picked up my monster, and I know now I can kill and survive. What a joke. My whole life. I had no sense of humor till now. Don't you agree? I could just throw my head back and my hands up and roar with laughter at the colossal joke of my life up till now. All those years of taking myself so seriously. All that struggle. That worry.

THE FIGURE: You're the best, Orestes. Do you not feel like the best?

ORESTES: I do. I am.

THE FIGURE: You're the brightest, finest, most aware and sincere.

ORESTES: I am tall. I am handsome.

THE FIGURE (*looking up in worship*): And I am with you. I am here.

ORESTES: I have killed my mother and there is no punishment.

(*He hangs suspended*, THE FIGURE *looking up in love and awe, as music begins.*)

THE FIGURE: For I am nothing without you. What am I without you?! For you are all. All. You are all, Orphan! Ohhh, Orphan, beautiful, beautiful Orphan.

ORESTES (*hanging amid the planets, the Godheads, the fragments of white debris, he starts to sing*):

> I wake up in the morning,
> The morning's aflame
> Lines of power mark my brain.
> In the morning sun awakening
> I wear a lion's mane
> In some magic corner of my brain.
>
> In this moment now reborn,
> I am tall and free,
> With nothing left to mourn,
> Orestes, Orestes, Great, Great Orestes.

THE SPEAKER (*in the dimness, she stands, looking upward,* THE FIGURE *beside her, but retreating, as she has her microphone and flashlight; beginning to speak, she uses her flashlight to pick out the Godheads hanging in the dark above her as if they are the planets of which she speaks*): There are nine planets moving around the sun—one, two, three, four, five, six, seven—

(*on seven she hits* ORESTES, *who now hangs among the other planets*)

—eight, nine—and the Earth . . .

(*the light, having hit* ORESTES *and moved on, now jumps back to him, as he hangs there humming the tune of his song*)

. . . is but one. Of the other eight, five have been known from prehistoric times. It would be difficult to imagine any planet less inviting than Jupiter—

(*her light flickers on planet three*)

but Uranus, Neptune and Pluto—

(*hitting heads four, five, and six*)

fill the bill. Only the Earth so far, has proven hospitable to man.

(*Her light holds on* ORESTES *for a beat.*)

And Mercury

(*planet one*)

completes its journey around the sun in far less time than Pluto.

(*Planet six. Then her light turns out.* ORESTES *hangs there, humming in a feeble light.*)

ORESTES (*singing*): Orestes, Orestes, Great, Great Orestes.

(*As his light goes to black.*)

The Orphan was first produced professionally by Joseph Papp on April 18, 1973 under the direction of Jeff Bleckner with the following cast:

THE SPEAKER	Jeanne Hepple
ORESTES	Cliff De Young
CLYTEMNESTRA ONE	Marcia Jean Kurtz
CLYTEMNESTRA TWO	Rae Allen
AGAMEMNON	W. B. Brydon
AEGISTHUS	John Harkins
GIRL	Mariclaire Costello
CALCHAS	Tom Aldredge
APOLLO	Richard Lynch
IPHIGENIA	Laurie Heineman
ELECTRA	Carol Williard
PYLADES	Peter Maloney

THE FAMILY MEMBERS:

FAMILY 1	Annemarie Zinn
FAMILY 2	Janet Sarro
FAMILY 3	Joanne Nail

Associate Producer, Bernard Gersten; set by Santo Loquasto; costumes by Theoni V. Aldredge; lighting by Tharon Musser; music by Peter Link.

The Orphan was produced in its current and final form by The Manning Street Actors' Theater of Philadelphia in association with the New York Shakespeare Festival produced by Joseph Papp on March 13, 1974 under the direction of Barnet Kellman.

THE FIGURE	Jon Thomson
THE SPEAKER	Cindy Winkler
ORESTES	Tommy Hulce
CLYTEMNESTRA ONE	Annemarie Zinn
CLYTEMNESTRA TWO	Norma Orazi
AGAMEMNON	Richard Fancy
AEGISTHUS	Mark McGovern
THE GIRL	Nancy Mette
ELECTRA	Bonnie Cavanaugh
IPHIGENIA	Maureen McFadden

THE FAMILY MEMBERS:

PYLADES	Alkis Papoutsis
BECKY	Susan Payne
SALLY	Pamela Sindaco
JENNY	Maureen McFadden

Associate Producers, Bernard Gersten and Joe Stinson; set by Debbe Hale; costumes by A. Christina Ciannini; lighting by James Leitner; music by Elizabeth Myers.

AFTERWORD: 1992

The prospect of writing an afterword for the four plays included in Volumes One and Two of *The Vietnam Plays* brings with it an inevitable surge of reflection. Quickly I'm back with thoughts of the war that spawned them. I'm also drawn toward the idea of assessing my work in the theater, my accomplishments or lack thereof. It's nearly inconceivable to me that more than twenty years have passed since I started to put these plays to paper. It was in the room I rented on the top floor of a residential home on Lancaster Avenue, near Villanova University. I was about to return to the Villanova graduate theater department at the time. I had been discharged from the army in 1967, after a two-year stint, one year in Vietnam with the 68th Medical Group, a headquarters unit overseeing evacuation and surgical hospitals.

The plays developed in a kind of symbiotic dance, each taking up certain aspects of my experience and my struggle to understand it. As they defined themselves individually, their emerging shapes somehow contributed to the development of the others growing around them. *Streamers* has the oddest history of them all. In a very concentrated several hours I wrote a one-act play with a working title of *Frankie*, which contained, in an abbreviated form, the first act of *Streamers*. What's odd is the fact that while it was the first of the plays begun, it was the last of the four finished.

Not long after writing *Frankie* I went to work on *The Basic Training of Pavlo Hummel*, and stayed with it until I had a draft of the complete movement of the play, though there would be a lot of fiddling and adding and subtracting to come. *Sticks and Bones* was then begun and brought to a similar point, where its nature was clear, though a lot more work was necessary. Under the title *Bones* it was given a very good production at Villanova, with James Christy

directing. A lot of the problems were sorted out, but many re-
mained. Somewhere during this period the first act of *The Orphan*
was written, as a long one-act called *Nor the Bones of Birds*.

By now I had nearly reached the end of graduate school. I was
sending work out and being turned down by an array of commercial
producers. Almost every institutional theater, including the Public
Theater, rejected *Pavlo Hummel* and *Bones*.

After leaving Villanova, in 1969, I went to work for the *New
Haven Register* as a feature writer. It was while in New Haven that
I one day plunged into my workroom, spellbound by an idea, and
came out four or five hours later having expanded the thirty pages
of *Frankie* into a sixty-or-so-page one-act that now included the
stabbing of the character Billy. The cause of this violence and its
nature was pretty much what it would remain. What was missing
and yet to come, though I didn't know it at the time, were the two
sergeants, Rooney and Cokes. A sergeant existed, appearing in the
early stretch of the text, but he did little more than show up, a sort
of stand-in for what was to come. Without the sergeants in their
large, almost mythical form, the scope of the play was narrow; the
metaphor of the title was absent, as was the coda that would
eventually end *Streamers* with a sense of mourning for a far larger
number of casualties than the two men who die before our eyes. It
was the sergeants and their stories that amplified the play, intro-
ducing a parade of men lost in one way or another, in one war or
another.

In New Haven I continued trying to arouse some interest in my
work. Somehow a producer/director read *Pavlo*. He found the large
number of characters prohibitive and he asked to see some of my
other work. My agents, James Bohan and Ellen Neuwald, gave him
Frankie. Almost immediately he phoned saying he wanted to do an
Off-Broadway production. This was 1969 or so, and evenings of
paired, thematically unconnected one-act plays were fairly common.
He suggested that I write another short play, or that he find one by
another author, but *Frankie* would be the centerpiece of the evening.
It was a strange, paradoxical moment. I remember clearly his en-
thusiasm, and the weird, apparently irrational certainty with which
I turned him down. I had no idea what was missing from the play as

it stood, but I knew it wasn't finished. I disliked the title and even the play itself in some way I couldn't define with any precision. My instinct in this matter was firm and would not let me proceed, even though, as an unproduced playwright, my hunger squealed in protest. Though I felt deprived, the contest was never substantial. I simply knew I couldn't allow the play to be produced in its present form.

Eventually *Streamers* would be completed, in 1974 or 1975, some seven years after its inception. Thousands of afternoons have slipped away from me in the intervening years, but I have a vivid, though impressionistic, sense of those hours. I don't know whether it was fall or winter or summer or spring; I think it was summer. But the place and the effort are clear. I had a little walk-up in Greenwich Village. My typewriter sat on the kitchen table beside the bed, a fold-out that had broken, dumping the mattress on the floor. The place was filthy. I was in the first phases of distress following my admission to both myself and my wife at that time that we were going to get divorced. I was depressed in a way that at times made it impossible for me to walk the width of my narrow room. I was often hung over, the TV blaring. And then I had this idea. I knew how to finish *Frankie*. Insight and intuition demanded that I get to work, but they were nearly sunk by the way I felt. I remember crawling from the bed to the table. I would type as long as I could sit up, which varied from fifteen minutes to maybe an hour. I kept at it for a full day, staggering back and forth, and when I was finished I had *Streamers*. The odd thing—or the oddest thing, perhaps, since much of this situation was certainly atypical—was the fact that when the struggle was over, the play was in a form that was almost final, word-for-word. When its production eventually rolled around in a year or two, there was very little rewriting to be done. The composition of this play consisted of a cumulative expenditure in hours of perhaps ten or twelve on three different days spread out over roughly seven years, and what I was left with at the end of all this was a text that needed only fine-tuning. With the metaphor of the streamer introduced, I had the title I'd been waiting for. This last rewrite was a matter almost exclusively of the sergeants and the various elements they brought into the play, the litany of rowdy, nearly prankish mayhem in the first act, dead men and daring men and failing parachutes, and the coda of absurdity and mourning with which the play would close.

The death of Sergeant Rooney defied the standard rules of proportion regarding cause and effect in dramatic development. For a while even those who liked the play wanted me to eliminate this stabbing and let the play climax with the murder of Billy alone, an event to which the text appeared logically aimed. But the addition of the sergeants and their stories in Act One, along with the story of the mythically absurd series of car crashes that opened the coda, created a context that embraced the horrible accident of Rooney wandering into the mayhem and dying before he ever knew what was going on. Suddenly the irrationality that had always lain at the core of the play had both a fundament and an embodiment; the buried themes and energies attained a full flowering. Violence, I had come to believe, is almost never conceptually or formally contained and limited to its appropriate, designated targets. In other words, it is not rational. It is not mechanical. The well-made play reflects the Newtonian clockwork universe. What I was after is more like nuclear fission in which the explosion of something miniscule unlooses catastrophic, ungovernable devastation. With the coda, Sergeant Cokes, ignorant of the fact that his friend is dead, mourns his own mortality and that of one haunting victim, a Korean who died at Cokes' hands, for whom he sings a lyric that is from no language, a kind of hymn to the chaos to which our lives are inherently subject.

By the time I had managed to complete a full-length version of *Streamers*, the other three plays, *Pavlo, Sticks and Bones*, and *The Orphan*, had all been produced. Even *In the Boom Boom Room* had been written and produced. *Pavlo* had been the first, with Joe Papp taking it on. Some of the details of this production are covered in the Introduction to the first volume of these plays, which was written to accompany the original publication of *Pavlo* and *Sticks and Bones*.

One of the ironies that comes back to me about Joe and the way he appeared in my life is that *Pavlo* and *Sticks and Bones* were both rejected by someone at his institution upon first submission. Though I should have had no hope that he would be interested in my work after such rejections, I remember deciding that I should resubmit to the Public. It made no sense and I have no explanation for my actions. A director, Mel Shapiro, who was interested in *Pavlo* asked me where I thought he should try to get the play done and I told him, "Joe Papp. The Public." A few weeks later the phone rang in my apartment in Drexel Hill, Pennsylvania, where I was living then, having returned to Villanova as a teacher. When I answered, the voice on the other end said, "David Rabe? This is Joe Papp." (I have to admit that writing these words I get a faint tingle and, for want of a better phrase, a threat of tears.) It's common knowledge in theatrical circles that Joe and I had troubles. And that's true; we did. As time went on, circumstances and our natures brought us into conflict, and looking back I don't really see anything that could have been done to avoid these altercations, disappointments, and rifts, nor diminish the harm they did us both as people and, more importantly I suppose, as producer and playwright. Given the two particular personalities that we were—and that's difficult to alter, since it's precisely the personalities that such an equation consists of—the dissension that ultimately emerged was inevitable. Though I struggled against it and was bewildered by it and tried to wish it away, I recognize and accept its inevitability now.

I also recognize that, in all likelihood, I owe my life as a writer to him. And as time goes on and I face the struggles of getting work produced, the probable truth of this notion is borne home again and again. My particular brand of playwriting suited Joe. The trouble was that we were people, and as people we were very different. There was a purity of anger and rebellion in Joe the producer, the director, the lover of Shakespeare, the artist, and there certainly was a matching aggression and rebellion in my work. For both of us the status quo was an unreliable, deceptive chimera, a fraud to be rent so that the thing it had been constructed to conceal could be let out. This was where we met and what we shared—a kind of vision.

But Joe was also compelled to possess, to assimilate, to put his stamp on things, and this was a tendency capable of generating negative consequences that counterbalanced his virtues, that threatened even to overshadow his virtues. Obviously most fledgling playwrights would find themselves vulnerable to the personality of someone in possession of the means to deliver plays to the public at will. I was not looking for a benefactor in the beginning, at least not in any conscious way. I was looking for a producer, I thought, and Joe had a theater dedicated to the production of new work. But he liked to function in a patriarchal way, and the possibilities available in the bounty of theatrical resources to which he was clearly proposing to give me access aroused in me a lurking filial response. So we would be father and son in some artistic way. But this is a relationship that is never simple, whatever its realm. More than most people, Joe and I should have known full well the perils and conflicts inherent in such an arrangement, and perhaps we did. Certainly we both had our needs, passions, neuroses, personalities, egos. His were expressed through the development of his institution, mine through my plays. While these two phenomena ought to have been able to thrive in concert, this wasn't always the case. When Joe declared that he was building his theater to do new plays, I imagined that he meant the needs of new plays were to be first in his hierarchy of priorities. *Each* play. One at a time, I thought. But this was not exactly the case. There was a second, buried premise tucked away inside that stated principle, and though it went without articulation it was more fundamental. It was a kind of reverse image, really, and in it Joe was doing new plays in order to build his institution. Interconnected and interdependent, these aims were not identical. The needs of the institution and any given play would not always be compatible.

We ended up on friendly terms, but our schism was an unhealed wound. We had failed and disappointed one another in the deepest way. We had failed at the work we had to do together—the work that brought us together and to which our lives were devoted. We spoke with some regularity during the final two years of his life. The last time was when he called me one morning; very close to death, as things turned out. He couldn't talk long. What I know now is that the only way things could have been different is if we were different people, and that's a futile proposition, a conundrum at best. But I was glad for the opportunity of those last conversations in which feelings and goodwill were shared.

One of the events that started us toward our breach was the production of *The Orphan*; not the production itself so much as the way it came about. In retrospect I can see that the factors that would eventually make our working relationship untenable were contained here in an elementary form. Or at least they were making their first appearance. The situation was full of contradictory and detrimental ingredients, the first and foremost being that the script was not ready and we all knew it. This was a matter that we openly discussed. The play had been performed at Villanova with some success but it was clearly unfinished. A further warning against the wisdom of staging it at this time was the mood of the director, Jeff Bleckner, who had directed successfully both *Pavlo Hummel* and *Sticks and Bones*. Jeff stated quite emphatically that he really didn't think he knew how to do the play. Furthermore, we were all tired. Or at least Jeff and I were tired. Joe I don't think was ever tired. So there we were, the playwright declaring the play unfinished, the director expressing confusion about his task, and the producer deciding that we would go ahead, that we must go ahead. Which was Joe's way, of course. The pause, the strategic retreat, the full stop to reflect were not within his normal scope.

By this time the Off-Broadway *Pavlo Hummel*, the Off-Broadway *Sticks and Bones*, and the *Sticks and Bones* on Broadway had all been mounted, in little more than a year. The television *Sticks and Bones* had been shot and edited and turned in to CBS. I was tired, and as we rattled in and out of Joe's office, struggling with our uncertainty about going ahead with *The Orphan*, I was increasingly convinced that what I needed was a chance to get away so that I might rest and write. And then one day our debates were disrupted by news that the airing of the TV version of *Sticks and Bones* had been canceled by CBS.

I had considered this development likely. Joe had made his contract with CBS contingent on their doing either *Sticks and Bones* or *Pavlo*. On the day the network executives informed us of their choice I had warned him that they had no idea what they were getting into with *Sticks and Bones*. In spite of the language problems in *Pavlo*, it was better suited for television. Still, when word of the cancelation came, I felt shocked and a little pummeled. As much as I might have been driven to write in a way that provoked tension between play and audience, the consequences were wearing me out. Joe, on the other hand, was energized by the prospects of a battle. He jumped from one fight to the next. That was his way, so he was ready to go. If he drew on the benefits of reflection before and after he acted, he found these moments like a fighter, in a clinch or crouching between rounds.

In an almost reflexive response we all felt a sense of urgency, a kind of moral obligation to stage *The Orphan* immediately. For Joe this call was absolute. At that time it was commonly believed that a theatrical production could have far-reaching effects in the "real" world, and we were tempted to feel that the repression of *Sticks and Bones* had to do with an attempt to block these effects. To the extent that *Sticks and Bones* and *The Orphan* were kindred, the banishment of one fairly demanded that the other step forward.

The end result was a scrambled, unfocused production of an unfinished play, which was almost universally condemned by the critical community. It was a bitter moment for me, because I felt that while the critics were correct in their judgment of the phenomenon they had been forced to witness onstage, there was a potential in the material that hadn't been protected and fashioned by anyone involved. I put myself and Joe at the head of the list—one day covering him with blame for commanding us to do the play and the next day rebuking myself for failing to resist him. In truth, the three of us had been moved by concerns irrelevant to the well-being of the play itself, along with a certain hubris about the importance of what we were doing. Once aimed and primed, we had seduced ourselves into action with the idea that we would solve the textual problems as we went along, discovering at the same time, we had hoped, authentic staging solutions. After all, we had done it before. But of course that never happened. Jeff and I were weary and the problems were extensive, particularly in the second act. To guarantee disaster, our haste and Jeff's uncertainty about how to stage the play led us to accept a floor plan for the set that frustrated a fundamental physical need throughout the play. The tub that was to serve as the site of Agamemnon's death and Orestes's birthplace was firmly planted in the downstage center of a gleaming oval floor. The flow of the play was strangled. Certain essential moves, the fluid cutting between widely separated locations and time periods, became impossible.

Once Agamemnon went into the tub he was stuck there in front of everyone. He had to climb in and out of the tub, walk on and off the stage, leaving the tub sitting there empty. A key mechanism was lost. Only later in a different production would a solution to this problem be found when a laundry basket on wheels was used as the tub. It swept in and out, bearing its victim or infant in it.

With *The Orphan* failing for the reasons that it did—at least as I saw them—I had my first bout of uncertainty regarding Joe's judgment and purposes. While I was reeling and retreating to Drexel Hill, he was charging ahead. But without me. Because while it was my only play at that moment, it was one of many for him. *The Orphan's* failure stung him, but he was achieving success almost simultaneously with other works opening in the numerous and multiplying chambers of the ever-expanding hive of his institution. Within months one of his biggest commercial and critical successes, *That Championship Season*, was to open. What I had glimpsed was that my benefactor, my patron, my artistic father, did not always have as his first priority the creation of the optimum circumstances for every play. His hierarchy of concerns was different than mine. He had theaters to fill, policies to devise and embody, campaigns to advance. I couldn't quite see how it was all working at the time. I knew that of course he had not only the right but the necessity to produce plays other than my own. Still, something nagged at me. Eventually I would come to understand the obvious: His first priority was always his institution. The institution needed to do plays and keep doing them, and to proceed according to a schedule that had to be met whether or not the best actors and directors were available for any given project. There is no other way for an institution to function. It needed the credits, the "product." It could afford failures as long as there was a seriousness of purpose along with a significant percentage of successes. There's an element of unpredictability about what creates a successful play and production anyway, and so a kind of shotgun method has its uses.

Looking back I can see that Joe loved my plays, and he loved me, but if there was a conflict between my needs or the needs of my play and the needs of his institution, he might feel torn but there was no uncertainty about what he would finally do. Such an obvious lesson, such a natural tendency, shouldn't have been so hard for me to grasp, but it was. I was much more concerned with the welfare of my plays than with the welfare of his institution.

Over the years three of the plays in these two volumes—*The Basic Training of Pavlo Hummel, Sticks and Bones* and *Streamers*—have come to be referred to as "The Vietnam Trilogy." But they were never that in my mind. There may have been a time when I spoke of *Pavlo, Sticks and Bones,* and *The Orphan* as a trilogy, because for a time I saw in them, or hoped to develop in them, three shifting but interrelated lenses onto the subject matter they shared. This was at that point when *Streamers* was still a long one-act and I was uncertain that it would ever mature into a fully developed play. As *The Orphan* approached its opening I seem to recall making some reference to a trilogy. The critical responses did, I think, describe *The Orphan's* failure as the failure of an attempted trilogy. What happened after that was that when *Streamers* came along and succeeded a few years later, the term was revived—with the success being substituted for the failure. By this time, however, the plays had become a foursome in my mind, a quartet. I felt *The Orphan's* failure—or at least the scope of that failure—had been primarily due, as I have already described, to the errors of the midwives. In the time between its first production and the arrival of *Streamers, The Orphan* had had a successful production with a radically revised second act in Winston-Salem, under the direction of Barnet Kellman, who had requested an opportunity to work on the play after seeing it in New York. He and I also did further work in a production in Philadelphia.

The play has never been reevaluated by the critical community, but my own faith in it has been heightened by a number of events, particularly a recent visit to Barnard College in New York, where in the spring of 1990 it was performed by students under the direction of Paul Berman. Before attending I sent a friend to scout the production and give me a sense of what to expect. Even though his report was encouraging, I was apprehensive as I took my seat. But what I saw was funny and scary and exciting. I was proud of the play, and was moved to take a final run at some slight textual modifications that have been incorporated into this book. The student actors and technicians were clearly ecstatic when I met them after the performance. The critic on the college newspaper went so far as to call the play a masterpiece. Now I recognize the need to temper my response to the judgment of a student critic, and even to the enthusiasm of the actors, I suppose. On the other hand, finding appreciation in a group of people who weren't even born when a play was written is about as close as a living person gets to enjoying the rewards of posterity. I'm willing to admit that my satisfaction here lacks the elements that commonly constitute sanctioned approval. I am also aware of the frustration inherent in my inclusion of these events in these pages. I'm simply choosing to accept as valid the enthusiasm of people working on and celebrating this play at the same time that I acknowledge their lack of "standard" credentials.

Which brings me back to where I started, the surge of reflection I felt regarding these plays, the war that led me to write them, and my accomplishments in the theater. Regarding this latter point I have to say that I've done far less than I thought I would when my first play was performed professionally. The reasons are many, but a basic explanation would have to be shaped around the fact that I never found a professional environment that made the production of plays efficient. Teamwork is demanded, but there are very few teams. The pressures are large and the conflicts of purpose and need are manifold. Egos collide behind the scenes and on the stage, creating huge trajectories of distraction that an audience can only experience but never understand. And everyone—each actor, the playwright, the designers, the producer, and the director—everyone is on their own, even as they meet in the midst of what ought to be a communal, interdependent, creative endeavor. I remember the shock I felt three days after the successful opening of *Pavlo Hummel* when I overheard an actor with a major part talking about how an audition had gone for him that afternoon. He was already looking for other work. This was common practice, I was soon to learn, born of necessity.

At Villanova University I had found fertile ground, but I was never able to find a professional equivalent. What made Villanova so vital was the fact that there was a community of people waiting to do the plays that I, along with the others writing there, could come up with. Partially it was the era, but it was also the fact that the chairman of the department when I arrived was a writer, Richard Duprey. There were skilled directors, Bob Hedley and Jim Christy, to name two. A number of talented playwrights appeared over the years, one of whom, Leslie Lee, has had many works produced in New York. But more importantly I can recall memorable scenes and full-length plays and productions and performances that were delivered by people who have since left the theater or never achieved a professional success but in that environment did remarkable work. There were pressures, but they were of a different, less insidious kind. New York was on the horizon, a goal, a dreamy something to be sought after, but it was in the future.

Today there is no real demand for plays in the New York theater. I remember the first time I came to New York and found fifteen or more serious plays running simultaneously on Broadway. They were a community in themselves, a neighborhood. Today there's a demand for "the hit of the season," for "the newest," "the best," "the greatest ever." I remember when, after my first plays had been done and while attending a Drama Guild function, I heard Robert Anderson say that New York playwriting was "a young man's game. They love virgins." At the time I took his meaning to be that playwriting demands a young man's energy, but he was saying something else. There's no demand for a body of work, though writers will be criticized for not having produced one. And there's no real interest in the true nature of the endeavor that must consist of work at differing levels of achievement. If you want to attempt a body of work, you better find a theater outside New York, as August Wilson has demonstrated clearly. The one exception I can think of to this rule is Lanford Wilson, who was prolific at the Circle Repertory. The dominant tendency, however, is for a writer to start out new each time, pretty much standing on nothing no matter what he might think his past accomplishments should have earned for him. The creation of a body of work by a writer demands a sense that each new creation is just that, the newest part of a living, developing entity in which imperfections are not only allowed but expected as necessary to the living process of development.

There's more to it, of course, in my case, as there probably is in everyone's, but this is a large factor. For me that first period of success, with all its satisfactions, brought with it concealed shocks, and it was exhausting. It became clear that the professional theater had perils in it, impediments that were widespread and unexpected and unclearly defined. Allies were needed, along with a method of working one's way forward, and I failed to find these things. Once such circumstances were discovered, I was obligated to forge or invent a way through them if I wanted to work in the theater to the extent that I thought I did. But I met this requirement with minimal success.

As for the way these plays relate to the Vietnam War, I guess I think they actually do embrace a portion of that inherently unembraceable subject. But there's something else that struck me as I reread them recently, and that is a subterranean level concerned as much with the state of things today as with the way things were back then. The core that animates them seems, at least to me, to emit a subtle but compelling light that in some strange way is as much prescience as it is reflection.

Since the end of the war the level of violence accepted as routine in this society has risen steadily, and there are times when I think that the war was the turning point, the launch pad that fired us into this lethal drift. At other times I see Vietnam less as a cause and more as a symptom of a comprehensive tradition of slaughter that must be understood as a constant in all history, ours included. In this mood Vietnam rises before me as our communal manifestation of an urge toward a shadowy savagery innate in all human character but with specifics reflecting the individuality of our society, the true assertion of our deepest, unacknowledged values. To surmise the existence of such a national disavowed appetite can feel almost obligatory given the sugary, sentimental veneer with which we dazzle and delude ourselves determinedly and incessantly, as if on the basis of a clandestinely established policy. What other desire, I wonder, could drive us to entertain ourselves with so much deception, with an endless barrage of images whose main criteria are that they must distract us and they must be false. What else could make us grow so petulant when we are forced to see anything but the most flattering, ingratiating, and moralistic of our fabricated reflections, if we are deprived of our happy endings.

And still, at those other moments when I stand convinced that the war was a pivotal, causative factor in our present situation, those years strike me as formative. I see them as a period of experimentation and development, and finally instruction. Then I am certain that the war, in its conduct and its subsequent denial, was a prototypic experience. It was an action indulged in and excelled at while being obscured by a spontaneous flare-up of mass denial, a kind of a self-imposed national amnesia and self-exoneration. From this unacknowledged negativity and confusion emerged our present chaos. Each evening on the network news we watched our leaders on full display as they struggled to escape the rubble of their own collapsing hypocrisy and culpability. Simultaneously we saw graphic depictions of the massive reach of war's destructive powers—body bags, burning villages, and ditches full of corpses. The poison was not so much that we did what we did as the way we denied that we were doing what we could see ourselves doing on television. Something in this schism cut the last moral tether by which certain ideals and urges and forces were balanced, and with their release and commingling the serial killer was hatched, the plague of drug dealers and child molesters and wife beaters, the corruption in government and business, the army of teenagers bearing guns through high school halls.

The truth is I know that the war didn't, in the common sense of the word, "cause" all this. But I believe that it was integral in the breeding of the arena we have come to inhabit. What I suspect is that as a nation we ended our adolescence with the war, and with this passage left behind the possibility of real "innocence" and true "goodness," with which we had been identified from our inception and to which we have refused to surrender our claims and addiction.

It's more than a little illuminating, I think, that following this period "deniability" was established as a desirable political goal. "Deniability." Think of it. Today "deniability" is openly acknowledged as an integral, an official, a requisite capability to be built into any well-designed governmental policy. "If I have to lie to live," says Ozzie in *Sticks and Bones*, "I will."

What I believe then is that these plays, if they address anything of significance, address this unmooring of our lives, this drift toward cynicism and impulsive violence. The humanity of the men wandering the nightmarish circumstances that gave Vietnam its identity is always present in the plays, as is the way its stress mixed decency and dutifulness, stimulating desperation and savagery and selfishness. Nobility marched with folly and ignorance. Innocence stood beside men who were petty, misguided, and mean. Fear and courage shared the night with sadism and heroism. A dizzying impression of being sent out on a compassless march pervades scene after scene. Each play is filled with a cast of men besieged by the suspicion that they are being duped by those who claim to lead them. They end up lashing out at peers meant to be their comrades.

The character Pavlo Hummel is a teenager ruled by a kind of crippled male ambition and need that somehow is drawn toward a rifle and violence as a way to fulfillment. It's a youthful energy, prone to action and anger and perfect for the military to appropriate in both its healthy and its distorted forms, toughening and ennobling the agent, or exploiting him, savaging him, and sacrificing him, all with fairly equal satisfaction.

It's interesting to note that when *Streamers* was first performed, the random violence it portrayed was not as familiar to us as it is now that numerous public havens such as Arby's and post offices and courthouses and day-care centers and school yards have been left dripping blood as sirens bear down in broad daylight. The war had barely begun before this phenomenon was given a full-blown incarnation with Charles Whitman climbing, rifle in hand, to his Texas bell tower. In Chicago, Richard Speck was preparing to advance with his knife on student nurses who he would terrorize and kill. Charles Manson, poised at the edge of his desert, awaited the summons of his madness. Apartment hallways had not yet turned into ambush sites. Stoops, street corners, and living rooms were only beginning to reveal the way they could regularly serve as slaughterhouses.

As *Streamers* reached its climax and transformed the homey little cadre room into just such an appalling site, the audience attending its first production in New Haven recoiled. They were certain that they should reject as alien the events unfolding before them. They wanted nothing to do with the play's claims of relevance and kinship.

The rage they were watching transformed before them like some mutating illness, a nightmare shape, dwarfing its carefully laid out predicates and restrictions. Mercilessly it dispatched its logical victim and then a bystander who had simply happened by to die in the surge of bloodshed about whose existence and appetite he had no warning. The human psyche distorts, this moment was saying, magnifying or shrinking everything it meets in a magical, illogical way and to an unpredictable degree. Less like the traditional, well-made models derived from Newtonian thought, it is more like the world of modern physics, defying mechanistic laws and measurements, eluding the grasp of reason and proportion.

With *Sticks and Bones* the poison of racism was portrayed as an intimate, inescapable presence in our national consciousness, as American as apple pie. Or perhaps it would be more apt to say, "our national unconsciousness." Arriving at its final image, the play faces us with a Vietnam veteran sitting in the living room of his home, his slit wrists bleeding into kitchen cookery provided by his mother. Before our eyes he is transformed into a grotesque, a zombie neither alive nor dead. Enfeebled and disenfranchised, he ought to be dead, yet he remains like some taxidermist's embalmed artifact, a kind of patriotic prop kept around to complete the family picture of wholeness, happiness, and absolute, beaming disconnection, while the Vietnamese girl, his companion and in some way the embodiment of the war, is strangled and put out of sight—stuffed in a garbage bag, or dragged behind the cheerily upholstered couch. Literally swept under the rug.

With *The Orphan* a number of these issues are revisited and not so much resolved as transmogrified and mythologized. These trends in the human psyche are viewed as ancient and eternal, as they return and evolve in order to reoccur "differently." In the end the mass murderer ascends from the abyss to the heights of an idolatrous cosmos, a rock star of sorts, a permanent member of our national array of icons, formed to suit the demands of the time that generated him while he, like his country, declares his perfect innocence. It's an icy ending, a youthful figure hovering alone in the deep, cold reaches of space itself, and to some extent it's counterpointed by the coda that closes *Streamers*, in which the absurdity, the carnage, and the ignorance are all embraced and mourned.

The Vietnam War, in its conduct and in the obfuscation proclaimed as its recognition and exegesis, was a seedbed, I think. A watershed. It was the swamp where history paused and could have shown us who we were and who we were becoming. In its flash and violence it was a probe into the depths, an X ray knifing open the darkness with an obscene illumination against whose eloquence we closed our eyes.